SIMPLE metalwork JEWELRY

LEARN BY DOING

CUTTING • PIERCING RIVETING & MORE!

JUDY FREYER THOMPSON

KALMBACH BOOKS

WAUKESHA, WI

Kalmbach Books
21027 Crossroads Circle
Waukesha, Wisconsin 53186
www.JewelryAndBeadingStore.com

Please follow appropriate health and safety measures when working with materials and equipment. Some general guidelines are presented in this book, but always read and follow manufacturers' instructions.

Every effort has been made to ensure the accuracy of the information presented; however, the publisher is not responsible for any injuries, losses, or other damages that may result from the use of the information in this book.

Published in 2016
20 19 18 17 16   1 2 3 4 5

Manufactured in China.

ISBN: 978-1-62700-250-9
EISBN: 978-1-62700-251-6

Editor: Dianne Wheeler
Book Design: Lisa Bergman
Technical Editor: Annie Pennington
Proofreader: Dana Meredith
Photographer: William Zuback

Library of Congress Control Number: 2016931493

Table of Contents

Introduction

Have you been wondering how to expand your jewelry horizons? Do you think you would love to create fabulous pieces of jewelry derived from manipulating metal by sawing, using shears, hammering, punching, dapping and using cold connections? If so, then this book is for you.

I will walk you through the basic tools you will need to start you on your way to metalworking; I will also touch upon tools available that you don't really need but would love to own!

There is something about forming metal by my own hand with something as simple as a plain hammer that never ceases to amaze and soothe my artistic soul. Turn the pages of this book for projects that provide basic, fun and easy-to-follow instructions if you are just starting out. If you are a seasoned artist, the projects are open for adding your own twist and details, limited only by your imagination. This book will walk you through the basic skills necessary to get started; once you have mastered the skills and projects in this book, you will be able to comfortably tackle more advanced metalworking techniques.

For all intents and purposes, the projects presented in this book will be made using copper, bronze, brass, aluminum, and nickel silver. All are user-friendly, relatively inexpensive, and their earthy compositions lend themselves well to a myriad of materials you can combine. Actually, once you master the techniques, you may wish to create a few of the projects in precious metals.

If you are ready to begin your journey, join me and let's have some fun!

Studio Area Safety

If you choose to set up a studio area in a livable space in your home, safety is even more important. A livable-space studio, although convenient, has the potential to be dangerous to pets or children. Always keep your tools out of the way of small hands; make sure chemicals are stored properly and in their original containers. If you mix up "safe" solutions such as salt and vinegar pickle, make sure to mark the vessel you store it in as to what is inside.

If you will be filing or sanding any material that will produce dust, wear a dust mask. I admit, not always comfortable, but it beats coughing or any potential health problems.

Tools, Tools, Tools!

Many of the tools I use in the projects are inexpensive. There are varied specialty tools available, but before investing in a tool that may be pricey, ask yourself how it will fit your needs. Is it used for only one specialty function, or will you reach for it many times?

I hope this book will provide you with the basic skills you were seeking to dive into metalworking and learn some new techniques to add to your repertoire. But most importantly, I want you to enjoy your journey and have fun!

Materials

Seemingly unassuming, sheet metal lends itself to jewelry making. Metal-cutting shears, a jeweler's saw, hammers, various pliers, and punches allow you to transform a one-dimensional piece of metal into a three-dimensional object. Once completed, you may choose to combine the sheet with wire, beads, fiber, or your own found objects to create a stunning piece of wearable art. You may also choose to add color by using a verdigris patina, liver of sulfur, or alcohol inks.

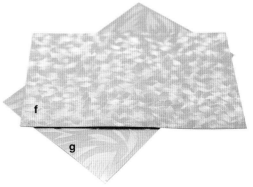

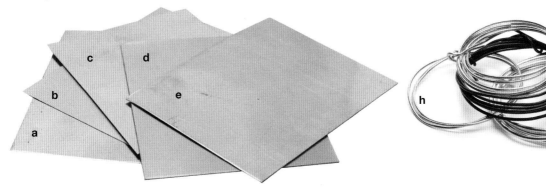

Metal Sheets

(a) Brass is an alloy made of copper and zinc. It has a bright, gold-like appearance. It is harder than copper, and is a bit more difficult to work with.

(b) Aluminum is a silvery-white colored element that is soft, lightweight, non-magnetic, and malleable. It is economical and easy to work with. Simply polished with fine-grit sandpaper, it can take on the appearance of silver.

(c) Bronze is an alloy comprised primarily of copper and tin and has a rosy tint. It is harder than pure copper, making it a little more difficult to work with.

(d) Nickel silver is also referred to as German silver and electrum. Named for its silvery appearance, it contains no "real" silver. Nickel silver is harder than copper, bronze, and brass, and in some instances, may be difficult to work with.

(e) Copper is a malleable metal. Pure copper (99%) is soft and easy to manipulate. It is easy to find and very economical, though not terribly strong.

Etched Sheets

(f) Etched copper sheets (pre-etched) are available, but making your own adds a personal touch to your pieces. Etching your own copper sheet is easy and economical, and of course, customizable.

(g) Patterned brass and copper sheets are available through jewelry suppliers, as well as craft stores. They lend themselves to mixing with plain sheet stock to add interesting detail to a piece.

Wire

(h) Round copper wire is available through jewelry suppliers ranging in size from 30-gauge (smallest) to 10-gauge. It is available in dead-soft and half-hard. Dead-soft wire is fully annealed (softened wth heat). Half-hard wire has been drawn down from a larger size wire and is about twice as hard as dead-soft wire.

(i) Dark, annealed steel wire is inexpensive and easy to find at home improvement stores. 19–28-gauge is often labeled "annealed steel wire," while 16-gauge steel wire is often sold as "rebar tie wire." Although the wire is labeled annealed, it is not as easy to work with as dead-soft copper of the same gauge.

(j) Round bronze wire is available through jewelry suppliers, ranging from 28-gauge (smallest) to 10-gauge. Although bronze wire is considered dead-soft, it will prove to be stiffer than dead-soft copper wire of the same gauge.

(k) Round aluminum wire is available through jewelry suppliers in diameters from 1/16" (approximately 6-gauge) to 3/16" and is considered dead-soft. It is also sold at home improvement stores where you can buy it by the foot, making it easy to purchase what you need.

TIP **If you purchase copper wire from a home improvement store, it is possible you will need to strip the insulation. Use a pair of wire strippers for this.**

Rivets and Eyelets

(a) Flat-head copper rivets are easy to install and they finish off smoothly. They provide a secure cold connection, and are found at jewelry and specialty suppliers.

(b) Round-head brass rivets are not only easy to install, but also provide an attractive finishing detail to a jewelry piece. These are easily found at jewelry and specialty suppliers.

(c) Copper eyelets are used to attach ephemera. Install them to reinforce a hole in which wear on fiber may be a concern, or simply to add an interesting element to a piece. Eyelets are offered in various finishes and are readily available at craft stores.

Copper Tubing

(d) ¼" copper tubing can be found at home improvement stores in 24" lengths, and is also available from jewelry suppliers. It can be cut with a jeweler's saw, and works great to make your own large-hole spacer beads.

(e) ⁵⁄₃₂" copper tubing works well for spacer beads, hinge pins, and toggle bars. It is easily cut with a jeweler's saw and is readily available from jewelry suppliers.

Findings

(f) Lobster claw clasps open when you push on a tiny lever. They come in many shapes and sizes, and are found in most craft stores.

(g) Earring wires can easily be purchased; however, it is more fun to make your own. A few commercially available styles are shown: French hook, kidney, and lever back.

(h) Jump rings are small circles of wire that are either open, soldered closed, or come with a split that can be twisted open and then closed. It's easy to make your own, too.

(i) Chain can be purchased by the foot or in pre-measured packages. It is available in many different link shapes and comes in various metals and finishes.

Tools

Basic metalworking does not require a huge investment in tools, materials, or time. You may already have an art space at home that could easily accommodate a few basic metalworking tools. If you are just starting out and need a space, your kitchen table is a fine place to start. Just make sure you clean it well so you are not mixing your work with your food! If you have a small area that will accommodate a sturdy desk, perfect. You'll need good lighting, a comfortable chair, and a tabletop to which you can attach a bench vise. Recycle tin cans to store small tools that tend to get buried on the top of your work space.

Embellishments

(j) Assorted beads can be used to enhance a metal jewelry piece. Coming in an array of colors and sizes, they can be easily found in craft stores.

(k) Spacer beads are usually metal or have a type of metal finish. They are often used to separate embellishments to present distinct details of a jewelry piece.

(l) Ribbon is often used as a kind of necklace to hang a metal pendant.

(m) Leather, while often used as a necklace for a metal pendant, can also be used to add a different texture to a metal project.

(n) Waxed cord is sometimes used in metal jewelry to add subtle detail.

Basic Tool Kit

This Basic Tool Kit contains tools and supplies to complete the projects in this book, although not all tools will be used in every project. I suggest you gather the tools you have and make a small investment in the ones you do not own.

A **1.8 mm hole punch** is often used with a chasing hammer to make holes in a metal surface.

A **4 oz chasing hammer** is often used for forming, flattening, and riveting.

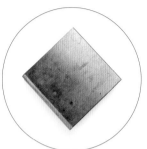

A **steel bench block** is a small work surface for riveting, texturing, and more.

A **bench pin and bench vise** are used to support a piece of metal or a piece of jewelry when sawing or filing is needed.

Flatnose or duckbill pliers are similar to chainnose pliers, but have straight outer jaws. This allows for holding pieces as bends are being made in metal and wire.

Roundnose pliers are critical for making loops and bends in wire. These pliers have tapered, conical jaws and are perfect for shaping wire.

Metal shears are similar to scissors, but are used for cutting metal sheets.

Wire cutters are pliers with sharp-edged jaws used to cut wire.

An automatic **center punch** is used to make a divot in metal that can be used as a guide for drilling holes.

A **hand file** is used to remove saw marks from edges and surfaces of metal. It can also be used to flatten edges and round metal corners.

Assorted grit sandpaper and sanding sticks are used for smoothing metal edges, removing file marks, and giving the jewelry piece a very fine finish.

A **spray sealant**, like a clear urethane (or a product called PYM II) is good to use when applying patina to a metal piece.

Also needed: **scissors, metal ruler, and permanent marker.**

General Tools

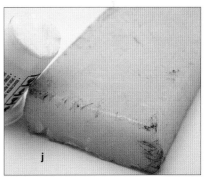

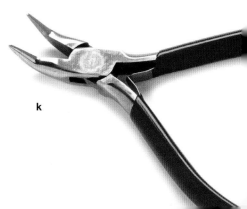

(a) A **jeweler's saw frame with a #1 or other size blade** is used to cut and pierce metal sheets. It is often used in conjunction with a bench pin.

(b) A **rawhide mallet** is often used for forming and flattening metal without marring it.

(c) Flush cutters leave less of a beveled edge when used to cut wire. One side of the cut will be flush, while the other side will be slightly beveled.

(d) A **4 oz. cross-peen hammer** can be used for adding interesting texture to various metals.

(e) A **16 oz. ball-peen hammer** can be used for adding texture to various metals.

(f) A **ring clamp** is used for holding small pieces of metal while filing, sawing, or finishing.

(g) Needle files (assorted shapes) are used to remove coarse file marks and to refine details on a piece of metal.

(h) A **flexible shaft or a pin vise** are both used to drill holes into metal. The flex shaft is available in economy models and has a foot pedal to control the tool. The pin vise is a hand-held tool that can be purchased at a home improvement store. You will need to use a bit more pressure with the pin vise in order to drill holes, but it is easy to control and is relatively inexpensive.

(i) Nail sets can be used for texturizing metals, making the appearance of tiny bubbles when struck randomly, and when setting round-head rivets.

(j) Beeswax or cut lube adds lubrication to saw blades and drill bits, preventing them from overheating, and prolonging their lives.

(k) Bentnose pliers are used to open and close jump rings.

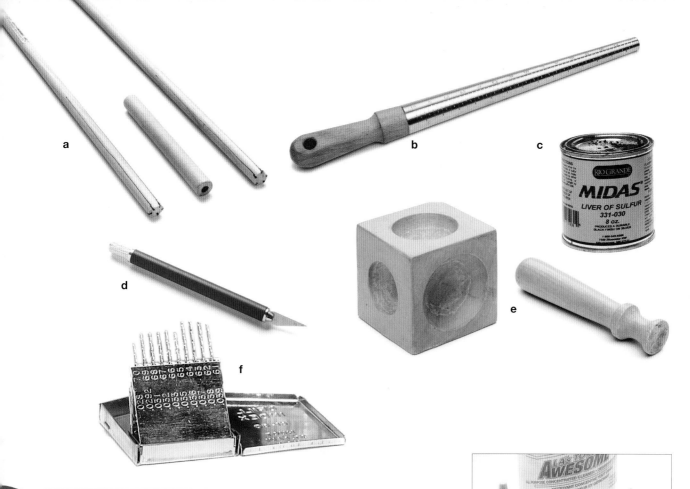

a

b

c

d

e

f

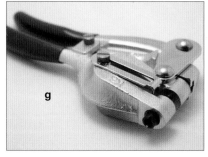

g

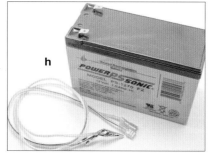

h

i

(a) Specific sized **mandrels** are available from jewelry suppliers, or you can use items found in your home: soup cans, wooden spoon handles, dowel rods, or prescription bottles.

(b) A **steel ring mandrel** is a great investment. It is indispensable for sizing rings and when hammering and forming is necessary.

(c) Liver of sulfur is a simple and relatively safe chemical patina for patinating a variety of common non-ferrous jewelry-making metals.

(d) A **craft knife** is necessary when using electrical tape as a resit when etching. Use it to cut out a design directly on the metal you will be etching.

(e) A **wooden dapping block and punches** are used together to create domed hemispheres with metal. They are great with textured metal, as they will not mar the metal surface.

(f) #52 drill bits are the most common size used for making holes in metal for the projects in this book. Different sizes of drill bits make it easy to get the true fit for rivets, eyelets, and other holes needed in a metal piece.

(g) A **power punch** is used in a lot of the projects to punch quick holes into metal instead of using a drill.

(h) 12-volt batteries with leads and connectors are manufactured for use in personal watercrafts and snowmobiles, and are relatively inexpensive. I'll show you how to use it to etch metal.

(i) Tacky Glue is made from a non-toxic formula, dries clear, and is water soluble. A **degreasing solution** is essential if you are applying patina or etching metal pieces. It is used to remove oils transferred to the metal from general handling. After using, wash the metal with plain soap and water, then rinse and dry thoroughly.

Cyanoacrylate adhesive, otherwise known as Super Glue, is a clear liquid or gel which bonds non-pourous materials, instantly.

Electrical tape strips placed on metal can serve as a perfect resist for etching. It can be cut easily with a craft knife.

1" painter's tape is used to mask off tools when using them during specific applications of an adhesive or to indicate a specific measurement on a tool.

earrings

Square Dangles

Who doesn't like bubbles? With my love of blowing bubbles, texturizing the square pieces of copper with various sized bubbles seemed to be just what they needed. Balancing the square shape with the bubbles adds a childlike feel to these earrings.

Skills
applying patina
dapping
hole punching
making earring wires
texturizing

materials
- **2** 1¹/₁₆" x 1¹/₁₆" 24-gauge copper squares
- 4" 20-gauge silver-plated wire

tools
- BASIC TOOL KIT **PG.8**
- Ball-peen hammer
- #52 drill bit
- Glass container
- Liver of sulfur
- Nail set (assortment)
- Pin vise (or flex shaft)
- Wooden dapping block and punch

13

1. File the edges of your copper pieces smooth, paying special attention to the corners. Use a 360-grit sanding stick to smooth the edges. Then use a 600-grit sanding stick for a finer finish **(Techniques, p. 100)**.

2. Texturize the squares on the steel bench block: With the ball-peen hammer, strike different sized nail sets to create a random bubble pattern **(Techniques, p. 98) (a)**.

3. Lay one square at a time, textured side up, in your dapping block's largest depression and curve the piece with a punch **(b)**.

4. Flatten one corner on each square using your flatnose pliers. (This will be where you punch or drill your hanging hole.) **(c)**

5. Punch or drill a 1.8mm hole in the top of each square ¹/₈" from the end **(Techniques, p. 99) (d)**.

6. Apply patina **(Techniques, p. 102-103)**.

7. Remove and wash the surface with dish soap and water. Rinse and dry, then lightly sand the copper using a 600-grit sanding stick. Rinse and dry a second time.

8. Make and attach earring wires **(Techniques, p. 108)**.

Preserved & Captured Ephemera Earrings

I thought ephemera referred to old printed paper, cards, and photos. It really means "printed paper to last for only one day," in other words the written word was meant to be read and discarded. Museums have curated and preserved ephemera for hundreds of years. In entomology, it refers to insects that hatch and live only one day, such as mayflies. Preserve ephemera to make a pair of earrings that last!

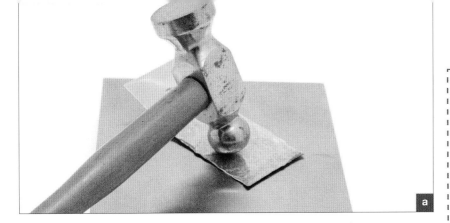

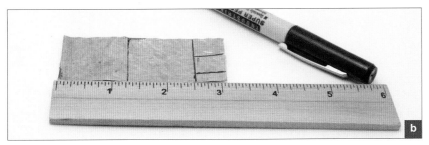

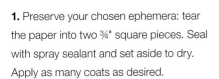

materials

- 1" x 2½" 24-gauge copper or bronze sheet
- 4" 20-gauge silver-plated wire
- **2** 0-80 x ¾" brass hex head machine screw with microbolt
- **4** 6mm outside diameter (OD) x 2mm inside diameter (ID) 2mm metal spacer beads
- **2** 10mm OD x 2mm ID 2mm thick spacer beads
- Ephemera
- Ribbon or leather scrap

tools

- BASIC TOOL KIT
- Ball-peen hammer
- Bentnose pliers
- Cyanoacrylate adhesive
- Heavy-duty wire cutters
- Liver of sulfur with glass container
- Spring clamp
- Wooden dapping block and punches

15

1. Preserve your chosen ephemera: tear the paper into two ¾" square pieces. Seal with spray sealant and set aside to dry. Apply as many coats as desired.

TIP **To help with tearing the edges of small pieces of ephemera, use a pair of bentnose pliers. These allow you to gently nibble away at the edges without removing too much material.**

TIP **After sealing, placing the pieces on plastic wrap works well to keep them from sticking.**

2. Texturize your metal sheet using the round end of a ball-peen hammer and a steel bench block **(Techniques, p.98) (a)**.

3. Measure two 1¼" squares and two ½" squares on a texturized metal sheet. Cut out with metal shears **(Techniques, p. 98) (b, c)**. Place each square on the steel bench block and hammer along each edge of each square to create an undulating edge **(d)**.

4. Find the center of each square and mark with a permanent marker. Use a center punch to make a divot at the mark and then punch through the piece using the 1.8mm hole punch **(e, f)**.

5. Measure ⅛" from one corner of one 1¼" square. Mark and punch with the 1.8mm hole punch **(g)**.

6. Clamp the two 1¼" squares together using the spring clamp. Punch a hole on the second square using the hole in the first square as a guide.

7. Smooth out the hammered edges with a 360-grit sanding stick. Follow with a 600-grit sanding stick to create a finer finish.

8. Lightly dap both sets of squares in the dapping block **(h)**.

9. Apply patina **(Techniques, p. 102-103).**

10. Remove and wash the copper surface with dish soap and water. Rinse and dry, then lightly sand using a 600-grit sanding stick.

11. Assemble the earrings as follows: microbolt, 6mm spacer bead, 10mm spacer bead, ½" square, leather or ribbon scrap, sealed paper, 1¼" square, 6mm spacer bead, hex nut **(i)**.

12. Tighten the microbolt using flatnose pliers. Do not overtighten **(j)**.

13. Using wire cutters, trim the shank to approximately 1/16" **(k)**.

14. File the shank with the metal file on the bench pin. Apply a drop of cyanoacrylate adhesive on the nut and shank to secure **(l)**.

15. Make and attach earring wires through the holes of each assembly **(Techniques, p. 108)**.

Articulating Triangle Earrings

Skills
cutting with shears
hole punching
riveting
making earring wires

This simple earring design uses 24-gauge copper triangle shapes you cut yourself. This particular pair of earrings finish off at 2", but they are easily customizable. The design offers a bit of a twist as the triangles are riveted together, allowing them to swing gently due to the space created during the riveting process.

materials

- 1" x 5" 24-gauge copper sheet
- **8** $\frac{1}{16}$" x $\frac{5}{16}$" flat-head copper rivets
- 4" 20-gauge silver-plated wire
- **2** 6mm beads

tools

- BASIC TOOL KIT **PG.8**
- Card stock
- Nail set (assortment)

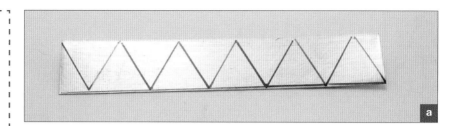

Triangle patterns

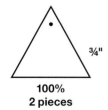

¾"

**100%
2 pieces**

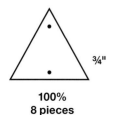

¾"

**100%
8 pieces**

1. Using a permanent marker, trace 10 triangle shapes onto the copper sheet **(a)**.

2. Cut the triangle shapes apart using metal shears **(Techniques, p. 98) (b)**.

3. Snip each corner of all of the triangles **(c)**.

4. Using a bench pin for support, round the corners with a metal file **(Techniques, p. 100) (d)**.

5. Using a ruler, find the center line on one triangle; make marks ⅛" from the bottom and top **(e)**.

6. Using a center punch on a steel bench block, make a divot on both marks.

7. Make a hole at each divot using the 1.8mm hole punch **(Techniques, p. 99) (f)**.

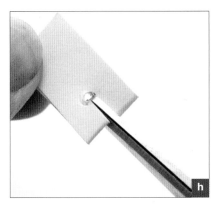
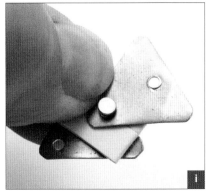
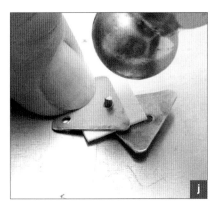

8. Using the first triangle as a pattern, align it individually with the shapes. Using a 1.8mm hole punch, make a top and bottom hole in seven more triangles. Punch only a top hole in the remaining two triangles.

9. Prepare your spacers by cutting 8 ¼" wide x 3" long pieces of card stock. Fold strips in half. Make a hole ½" from the folded end with the 1.8mm hole punch **(g)**.

10. Using scissors, carefully cut a slit from the folded end to the punched hole **(h)**.

11. Insert a rivet through the center hole in one triangle. Then place the paper spacer on the shank, followed by the top hole in a second triangle **(i)**.

12. Set the rivet using a chasing hammer **(j)**.

13. Finish the back of the rivet by using a file to round off the rivet shank **(Techniques, p. 100) (k)**.

14. Remove the paper spacer.

15. Repeat process to make two five-triangle components.

16. Make and attach earring wires to the top hole of each assembly **(Techniques, p. 108)**.

Arrowhead Earrings

Native Americans made many fantastic tools, one being the arrowhead. These earrings closely resemble arrowheads carved from flint. Nickel silver is very hard, therefore be prepared to break a blade or two. Using the thicker metal allows for a nice, textured edge when using a round file. Adding a small fiber detail is reminiscent of how the craftsmen secured the arrowhead to the handle of a spear or arrow.

Skills
filing & sanding
making earring wires
piercing
sawing
texturizing

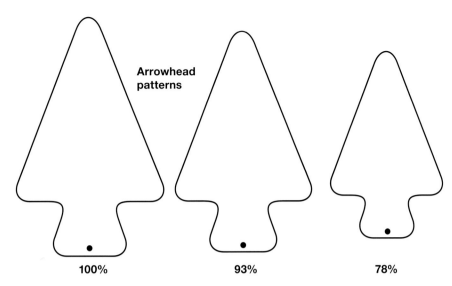

Arrowhead patterns

100% 93% 78%

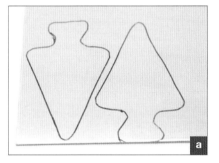

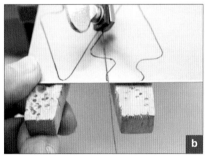

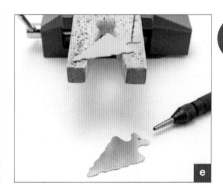

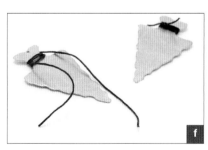

TIP **20-gauge nickel silver is a very hard metal. Be prepared to break a couple of blades. You could use thinner-gauge metal, but thinner will not show the edge detail as well.**

1. Using a pencil, draw the shape of the arrowhead on the index card. Cut out the paper pattern and transfer it onto the nickel silver sheet twice **(a)**.

2. With a jeweler's saw and #1 blade, cut out both shapes, resting the work on a bench pin **(Techniques, p. 104)**. *(No need to match exactly; you will be texturizing the edges.)* **(b)**

3. Grasp one shape with the spring clamp. This will serve as a handle while you are filing and adding details.

4. Apply beeswax (or cut lube) to the round file. With the piece supported on a bench pin, use the file to make gouges around the edges, pushing the file away from you and moving in only one direction **(c)**.

5. Tear off a small piece of 240-grit sandpaper and use it to make swirl marks on the front and back of the arrowhead pieces **(d)**.

6. Make a divot in the center of the bottom of each arrowhead with a center punch. Drill holes with a #52 drill bit in a pin vise (or flex shaft) **(Techniques, p. 98) (e)**.

7. Use a 360-grit sanding stick to smooth. Then use a 600-grit sanding stick for a finer finish **(Techniques, p. 100)**.

8. Wrap the waxed cord around the tang and tie off using a square knot. Apply a dot of cyanoacrylate adhesive to secure the knot **(f)**. Trim the ends.

9. Make and attach earring wires to each arrowhead **(Techniques, p. 108)**.

Retro Paisley Pattern Earrings

Paisley patterns are mesmerizing! These earrings are reminiscent of the fantastic patterns from the 60s. Aluminum sheet stock is cut in a paisley pattern, texturized, and embellished with a bit of sparkle in the middle. Adding shoe polish will highlight the texturized pattern.

Skills
filing & sanding
inserting eyelets
making earring wires
sawing
texturizing

22

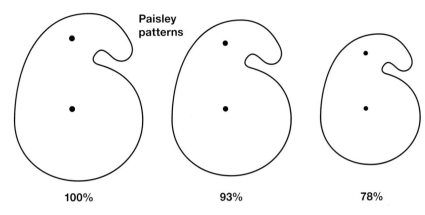

Paisley patterns

100%   93%   78%

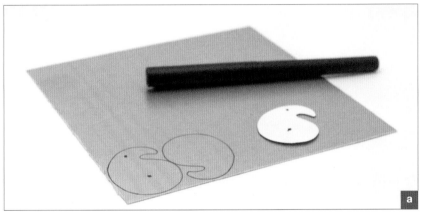

a

1. Draw the design on an index card. Cut out and transfer the design to the masked side of the aluminum sheet using a permanent marker. Trace twice. Mark the hole locations on one piece with a marker **(a)**.

2. With jeweler's saw and #1 blade, cut out both shapes **(Techniques, p. 104)**.

3. Use a center punch to make divots at both hole locations on one shape **(b)**.

4. Punch holes using 1/8" power punch (or drill with 1/8" drill bit) and pin vise (or flex shaft **(Techniques p. 99) (c)**.

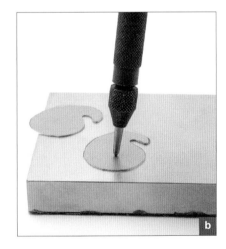

b

c

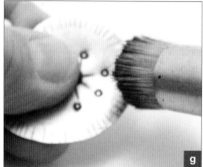

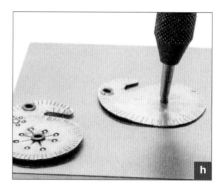

5. Remove the masking from both shapes. Clamp them together with the spring clamp, and file the edges smooth with a metal file **(Techniques, p. 100) (d)**.

6. While the shapes are clamped together, use the punched shape as a pattern to punch the holes in the second shape. (See step 3.)

7. Using a permanent marker, draw the pattern you want to stamp. Lay the pieces on a steel bench block and add embossed details with a ¹⁄₃₂" nail set and flat-head screwdriver **(e)**.

TIP **Wear eye protection! Screw-drivers aren't designed to be struck with a hammer and can shatter.**

8. Using a pair of wire cutters, texture the edges as shown. *(Don't cut all the way through the metal.)* Flatten if necessary using a rawhide mallet on your steel bench block **(f)**.

9. Refine edges if necessary after embossing the edges. Clean off marker with isopropyl alcohol.

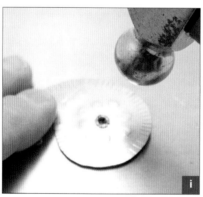

10. Lightly sand the surface with 600-grit sandpaper.

11. Using a paint brush or cloth, rub black shoe polish on the shapes, paying close attention to the stamped areas **(g)**.

TIP **Trim the bristles of a paint brush to approximately ½". This will make the bristles stiffer and will allow you to embed the shoe polish more easily.**

12. (I used an embossing heat gun to set the color quickly. You can let it air dry.) Rub off excess shoe polish with a soft cloth.

13. Insert the eyelets through a hole with the finished end on the stamped surface. Use a center punch on the steel bench block to start flaring the end **(h)**.

14. Gently hammer to complete flaring using the chasing hammer **(Techniques, p. 101) (i)**.

15. Use a spray sealant to seal the color.

16. Apply a dot of cyanoacrylate adhesive to the rhinestones and secure in the center of the eyelet **(j)**.

17. Make and attach earring wires to each paisley **(Techniques, p. 108)**.

Copper Foil Earrings

I was so excited to be gifted with a roll of copper foil from a family friend; oh, the possibilities! Using copper foil gives you a beautifully patterned finish, different from basic texturizing. You can vary the size and dress them up a bit by using embellished earring wires if desired.

Skills
applying copper foil
cutting with shears
filing & sanding
hole punching
texturizing

materials

- 2" x 1¼" 24-gauge copper sheet
- 4" x 4" .06mm copper foil
- 4" 20-gauge silver-plated wire
- **2** 6mm beads

tools

- BASIC TOOL KIT **PG.8**
- Cyanoacrylate adhesive
- Painter's tape
- Spring clamp

Ellipse pattern 100%

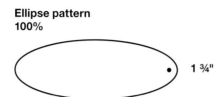

1 ¾"

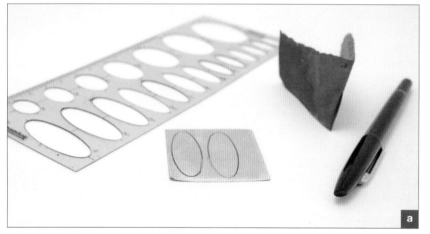

a

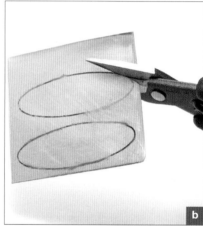

b

TIP **Copper foil is available online from sellers on Ebay. It is also widely available at any building supply store and some craft stores.**

1. Trace a 1¾" ellipse shape on the copper using the pattern and a fine point permanent marker **(a)**.

2. Cut out the shapes with metal shears **(Techniques, p. 98) (b)**.

3. Use a spring clamp to clamp the pieces together. Then use a metal file to smooth the edges. Use the bench pin for support **(Techniques, p. 100) (c)**.

4. Roughup one side of each shape with 360-grit sandpaper. (This will create some "tooth" for the adhesive.)

5. Using scissors, cut a piece of foil approximately 2" x 2". Remove the backing and crumple lightly. (Avoid making a ball, as the intention is to keep the foil relatively flat and create ripples.)

Using only your fingers, apply light pressure to flatten the foil. Repeat with a second piece of foil **(d)**.

6. Apply a bead of cyanoacrylate adhesive down the center of one copper ellipse shape (roughed-up side) **(e)**.

7. Carefully press the prepared foil onto it to secure. Repeat with the other shape and set aside to dry **(f)**.

8. When the first application of adhesive is dry, trim the excess foil with scissors **(g)**.

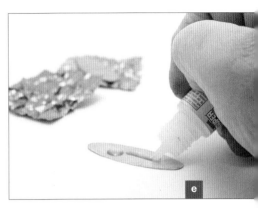

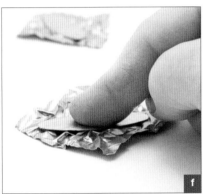

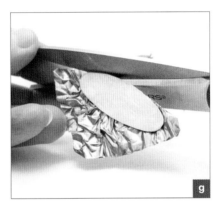

9. Wrap the flatnose (or duckbill) pliers with one layer of painter's tape. Working along one edge at a time, carefully dab adhesive between the foil and the copper, then squeeze the flatnose (or duck bill) pliers. When dry, repeat on the other side. Flatten the foil evenly to compress the ripples **(h)**.

TIP **Apply sparingly and on one edge at a time to avoid excess adhesive.**

10. When the adhesive is completely dry, smooth the edges with a 360-grit sanding stick, then use a 600-grit sanding stick for a finer finish **(Techniques, p. 100)**.

11. Align one shape on the pattern, using the permanent marker to locate the earring wire hole centered ⅛" from one end **(i)**.

12. Use a center punch and a steel bench block to make a divot at the mark **(j)**.

13. Make a hole at the divot using a 1.8mm hole punch. Line up the second ellipse, smooth sides together, and punch a hole through the second piece **(Techniques, p. 99) (k)**.

14. Seal if desired with spray sealant.

15. Make and attach earring wires to each ellipse **(Techniques, p. 108)**.

Pendulum Earrings

This project will show you how to transform two flat ellipse shapes into a pair of pendulum-shaped earrings reminiscent of the pendulum on a Grandfather clock. I cut these from a piece of etched copper, then made two short lengths of chain to suspend them from.

**Ellipse pattern
100%**

2"

materials
- 2" x 4" 24-gauge etched copper sheet
- 16" 18-gauge wire
- 4" 20-gauge silver-plated wire
- **2** 3mm beads
- **2** 5mm copper spacer beads

tools
- BASIC TOOL KIT **PG.8**
- 12mm mandrel pliers
- Brass brush
- Degreasing solution
- Flush cutters
- Liver of sulfur with glass container
- Painter's tape
- Spring clamp

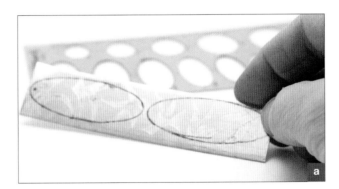

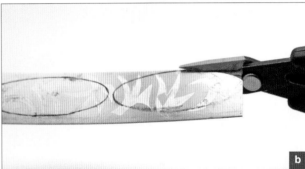

1. Trace two 2" ellipse shapes on the etched copper using the ellipse pattern and a fine point permanent marker **(a).**

2. Use metal shears to cut out the shapes **(Techniques, p. 98) (b)**.

3. Use a spring clamp to clamp the pieces together. Then use a metal file to make the edges smooth. Use the bench pin for support **(Techniques, p. 100) (c)**.

4. Measure 1/8" from each end of the 2" shapes and mark with a permanent marker **(d)**.

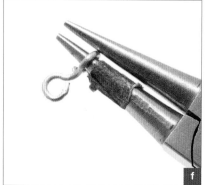

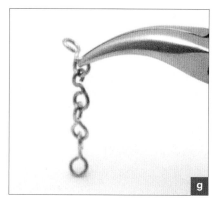

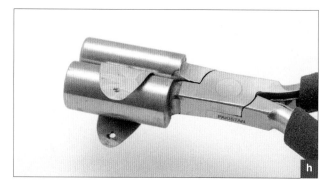

5. Using a center punch and a steel bench block, make a divot at the mark **(e)**.

6. Make holes at the marks using a 1.8mm hole punch **(Techniques, p. 99)**. Sand edges smooth using a 360-grit sanding stick.

7. Sand the length of 18-gauge wire with 600-grit sandpaper, then cut 16 pieces of wire 1" long. File the ends flat using the metal file.

8. Using a ruler, make a mark on the roundnose pliers at 3mm and wrap with a piece of painter's tape.

9. Using this mark as a reference, form a plain loop on one end of a piece of wire. Then form a perpendicular plain loop on other end **(Techniques, p. 109) (f)**.

10. Assemble the chain into four 4-link lengths. Straighten and adjust the loops to make sure they are closed completely and perpendicular to one another **(g)**.

11. Bend the ellipse shapes around the 12mm mandrel pliers, making sure the etched sides face out **(h)**.

12. Attach one chain to each end of each formed ellipse **(i)**.

13. Degrease the earrings and rinse thoroughly.

14. Apply patina **(Techniques, p. 102-103)**.

15. Remove and wash the surface with dish soap and water. Rinse and dry, then lightly sand using 600-grit sanding stick. Rinse and dry a second time. Gently buff the components using the brass brush.

16. Bring the chains together and attach to earring wires **(Techniques, p. 108) (j)**.

Riveted Aluminum Earrings

This simple earring project will have you using a heavy hammer to add dimension to aluminum wire, drilling holes, and inserting rivets for accent. Adding a chunky bead to the earring wire completes these statement earrings. These earrings can easily be made longer if you desire. Simple, but elegant!

Skills
drilling
filing & sanding
making earring wires
riveting
sawing

31

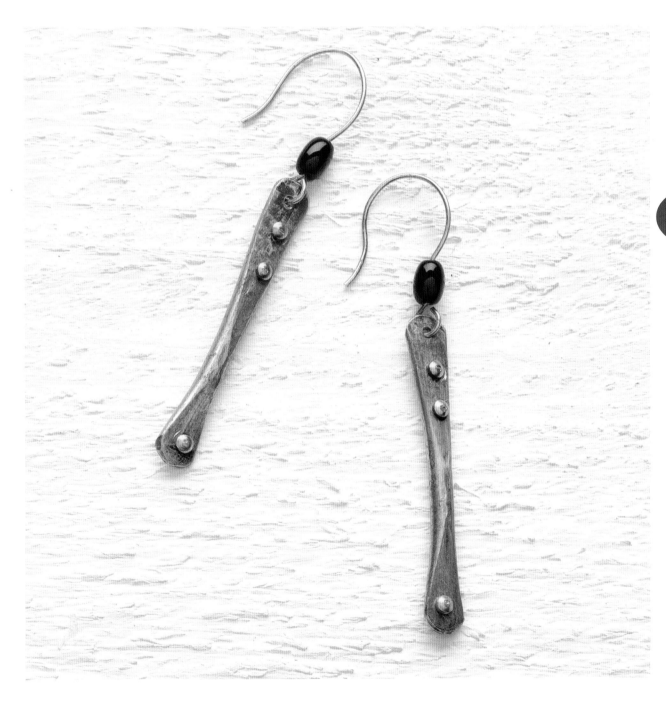

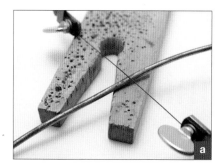

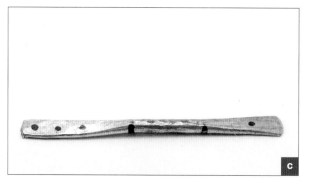

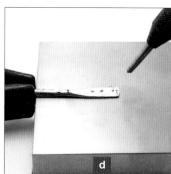

materials

- 5" 8-gauge aluminum wire
- 4" 20-gauge silver-plated wire
- 2 chunky accent beads
- 6 $\frac{1}{16}$" x $\frac{5}{16}$" round-head brass rivets

tools

- BASIC TOOL KIT **PG.8**
- #52 drill bit
- Ball-peen hammer
- Beeswax (or cut lube)
- Jeweler's saw and #1 blade
- Nail sets (assortment)
- Pin vise (or flex shaft)
- Spring clamp

32

TIP Aluminum is an excellent thermal conductor, so you can use a spring clamp on one end of the wire during hammering and drilling to prevent your fingers from getting hot.

1. Measure and mark two 1½" pieces on the 8-gauge aluminum wire with the permanent marker. Cut the wire at each mark using a jeweler's saw and #1 blade **(Techniques, p. 104) (a)**.

2. Measure and mark 1" from one end and ¾" from the other end.

3. Holding one end of a wire with the clamp, rest the wire on the steel bench block, and use the flat end of the ball-peen hammer to flatten the opposite end. Although aluminum is quite malleable, you will need to put some muscle into hammering this gauge of wire. Hammer until you reach the mark made. Flip and flatten the other end. Aim for approximately a 2mm thickness. Repeat with the other wire **(b)**.

4. Using the metal file, round off the edges, resting the wire on the bench pin for support. Make sure both wires match in length **(Techniques, p. 100)**.

5. Measure ⅜" from the ¾" flattened end and mark with the permanent marker. Measure ⅛", ⅜", and ⅝" from the 1" flattened end and mark using a permanent marker **(c)**.

6. Using the center punch, make a divot at each marked location **(d)**.

7. Again, clamp one end of the wire and rest the wire on the bench pin. Apply beeswax (or cut lube) to the #52 drill bit and drill holes at each divot with a pin vise (or a flex shaft) **(Techniques, p. 98) (e)**.

8. Using the 360-grit sanding stick, sand the wires and make sure all edges are smooth.

9. Clamp the nail set in the bench vise and set the rivets in three places on each wire **(Techniques, p. 101)**. The hole closest to the end will be for attaching the earring wire **(f)**.

10. Feel for burrs on the rivets. If found, use the sanding stick to smooth over.

11. Using a modified 27mm interlocking block ear wire jig, make two earring wires **(Techniques, p. 108)**.

Hammered Triangle Earrings

Using aluminum for these earrings gives the appearance they were made from silver. They are incredibly lightweight therefore easy to wear. By varying the bead dangles, you can change the feel of the earrings from having a bit of bling to having an earthy feel.

Skills
cutting with shears
filing & sanding
hole punching
making earring wires
texturizing

**Triangle pattern
100%**

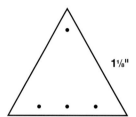

1⅛"

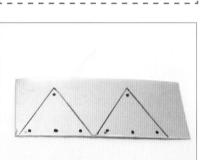

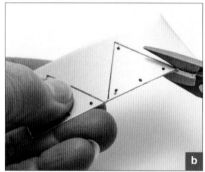

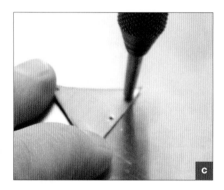

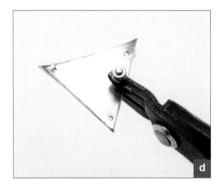

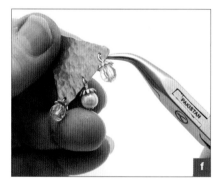

1. Trace two 1⅛" triangle shapes on the protective coating on the aluminum sheet. Make a mark in each corner of the triangles, ¹⁄₁₆" from each edge. Make a mark centered on one edge **(a)**.

2. Cut out shapes using metal shears **(Techniques, p. 98) (b)**.

3. Using the center punch, make a divot at each mark **(c)**.

4. Punch holes using a 1.8mm hole punch **(Techniques, p. 99) (d)**.

5. File sharp edges with a metal file using the bench pin for support. Use a 360-grit sanding stick to smooth. Then use a 600-grit sanding stick for a finer finish **(Techniques, p. 100)**.

6. To add texture, hammer the pieces on a steel bench block using the ball side of a chasing hammer. Flip and flatten with the flat side of the hammer **(Techniques, p. 98) (e)**.

7. String a 6mm bead and a bead cap on a headpin to make one dangle. Repeat twice. Make a simple loop at the top of each headpin.

8. Place the bead dangles in the three lower holes using bentnose pliers **(f)**. Make a second earring.

9. Make and attach earring wires to each triangle **(Techniques, p.108)**.

Triangle Earrings with Rivets

Like the feel of the aluminum earrings, but prefer a more "industrial" look? Replacing the bead dangles with brass rivets gives a totally different style.

materials
- 2"x 3" 24-gauge aluminum sheet
- 4" 20-gauge silver-plated wire
- **6** $^1/_{16}$" x $^5/_{16}$" round-head brass rivets
- **2** 4mm crystal beads

tools
- BASIC TOOL KIT **PG.8**
- $^3/_{32}$" nail set

Trace the triangle pattern and then follow steps 1–3 from the Hammered Triangle Earrings project.

9. Punch three rivet holes using the 1.8mm punch **(Techniques, p. 99) (a)**.

10. File sharp edges with a metal file using the bench pin for support **(Techniques, p. 100)**.

11. Clamp the nail set in the bench vise and insert the rivets in the three holes at the bottom of each triangle **(Techniques, p.101)**.

12. Use a 360-grit sanding stick to remove any burrs on the rivets. Then use a 600-grit sanding stick for a finer finish **(Techniques, p. 100)**.

13. Make and attach earring wires **(Techniques, p. 108)**.

bracelets

Endless Circles Bracelet

This project will show you how to quickly and easily turn a dozen copper washers into an interesting bracelet. You will drill or punch the washers, overlap them, and install a rivet. This bracelet looks great no matter if you decide to leave it natural, keep it polished, or apply a patina.

Skills
applying patina
drilling
filing & sanding
hole punching
riveting

materials

- **12** 1" outside diameter (OD) copper washers
- **12** ¹⁄₁₆" x ⁵⁄₁₆" diameter flat-head copper rivets

tools

- BASIC TOOL KIT **PG.8**
- Degreasing solution
- Soup can

Circle pattern 100%

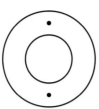

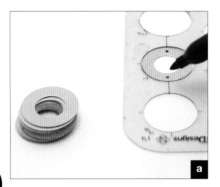

1. Using the circle pattern, mark holes on one washer at 12:00 and 6:00 **(a)**.

2. Using a 1.8mm hole punch, make holes at the two locations marked on one washer. Use the first washer as your guide and punch holes in the remaining washers **(Techniques, p.99) (b)**.

3. Sand each washer using 600-grit sandpaper.

4. After sanding, degrease the washers and rinse with plain water.

5. If you choose, apply the salt and ammonia patina to the washers **(Techniques, p. 102)**.

6. After your patina is done, or if you wish to keep the bright copper color, hang the washers by individual scraps of wire and apply one light coat of spray sealant.

7. Once the sealant is dry, start assembling your washers. Using a chasing hammer and steel bench block, rivet one washer to another **(Techniques, p. 101) (c)**.

8. Continue to rivet the washers together, overlapping each washer in the same direction **(d)**.

9. Prior to setting the last rivet, use your fingers to bend the bangle around a soup can. This will coax the washers into the shape of a bangle **(e)**.

10. Set your last rivet. Make sure all of your rivets are smooth with no burrs. Use a 360-grit sanding stick to smooth any rough areas. Then use a 600-grit sanding stick for a finer finish **(Techniques, p. 100)**. Adjust the bangle as needed to form a perfect circle **(f)**.

11. Spray the entire piece with sealant and let it dry.

Patterned Bangle

Combining patterned copper jewelry wire and patterned brass sheet stock proves to create an attractive bangle bracelet. Since the pieces are cut to length, it is really easy to make this bracelet to your desired size. Rivets hold it all together!

Skills
cutting with shears
filing & sanding
drilling
hole punching
riveting

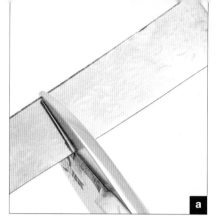

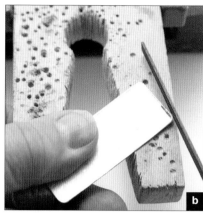

materials

- 6" 1.3mm x 5.3mm 16-gauge patterned copper wire
- 1½" wide x 4" long 24-gauge patterned brass sheet
- 12 ¹⁄₁₆" x ⁵⁄₁₆" copper rivets

tools

- BASIC TOOL KIT **PG.8**
- #52 drill bit
- Beeswax (or cut lube)
- Bracelet mandrel
- Pin vise (or flex shaft)
- Rawhide mallet
- Soup can
- Spring clamp

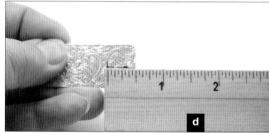

40

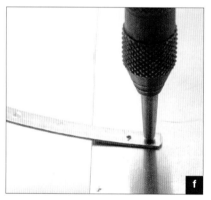

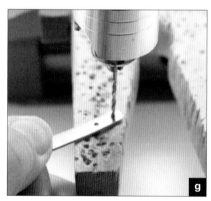

1. Measure and mark three ¾" wide by 2" long rectangles on the backside of the patterned brass sheet. Cut out using metal shears **(Techniques, p. 98) (a)**.

2. Using the metal file, file the edges smooth and round the corners. (Support the brass sheet with a bench pin.) **(b)**

3. Measure three 2" long pieces of patterned copper wire and cut them using metal shears.

4. Using the metal file, file the edges on the copper wire smooth and round the corners slightly. (Support the jewelry wire with a bench pin.) **(Techniques, p. 100) (c)**.

5. Measure and mark ½" from each end of the brass sheets. Locate the center line and mark with the permanent marker **(d)**.

6. On the backside of the copper wire, measure ⅛" and ⅜" from each end. Mark with the permanent marker in the center of the wire **(e)**.

7. Using the center punch and steel bench block, make a divot at each mark on the copper wire **(f)**.

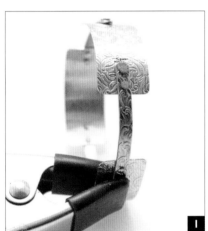

8. Drill all holes using a pin vise (or flex shaft) with a #52 drill bit. Use beeswax (or cut lube) to lubricate the drill bit. Use a bench vise and bench pin to support the copper wires **(Techniques, p. 98) (g)**.

9. Position one piece of copper wire at the ½" mark and centered on a brass piece. Hold the pieces in place with a spring clamp **(h)**.

10. Drill one hole in the brass piece with a pin vise (or flex shaft) and #52 drill bit **(i)**.

11. Insert one rivet from the copper wire side. Trim and set the rivet using the chasing hammer and steel bench block **(Techniques, p. 101)**. Use a hole in the copper wire as a guide **(j)**.

12. Move to the next piece of brass; clamp, drill, and set one rivet as in step 11.

13. Continue until you have set one rivet in each, creating a long, straight strip. Be sure to leave the ends free.

14. Set the remainder of the rivets, making sure the copper wire is straight.

15. Begin to bend the assembly around the soup can **(k)**.

16. When a slight bend has been achieved, use the spring clamp to hold the jewelry wire in place **(l)**.

17. Drill and set the remaining two rivets.

18. Slide the bangle onto the bracelet mandrel and continue to shape it using a rawhide mallet **(m)**. Use finishing techniques like sanding and sealing if needed.

Copper Foil Bracelet

Turn a flat sheet of copper into a gorgeous bracelet using copper foil which gives you a beautifully patterned finish different from texturizing. An etched interior adds an interesting hidden detail. Using a 16-gauge bracelet blank adds a spring to the cuff part and keeps tension on the handmade chain and hook clasp. The addition of eyelets add a layer of protection to the copper foil.

Skills
applying patina
etching
filing & sanding
inserting eyelets
making Figure-8 links

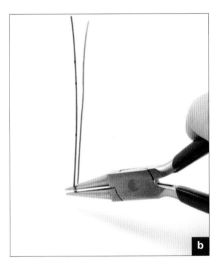

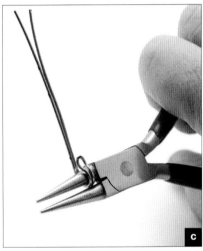

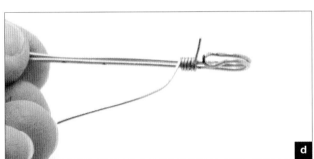

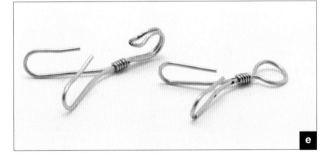

1. Prepare the copper strip for etching by sanding the surface with a 600-grit sanding stick **(Techniques, p. 100).** Round off sharp edges with a metal file. Degrease, rinse with water, and dry thoroughly.

2. Apply electrical tape to one side of the strip. Print a design or free cut directly on the tape. If you have printed a design, use Tacky Glue to adhere it to the tape.

3. Using a craft knife, cut out the part of the design you wish to see etched. Etch the strip **(Techniques, p. 99) (a)**.

4. Remove remaining paper and the cut-out tape resist and thoroughly clean the strip. Set aside.

5. Clean all copper wire with a 600-grit sanding stick. Cut one piece of 18-gauge wire 4¼" long and one 5½" long. File ends flat with a metal file. Make a 7mm loop in the middle of the 4¼" wire **(b)**.

6. Make a 2mm loop in the middle of the

5½" wire. At the bend, make a slightly upturned bend with roundnose pliers; then grasp above the upturned end with roundnose pliers and make a hook **(c)**.

7. Wrap the 20-gauge wire five times just below the hook you made in the 5½" long ends of the 20-gauge wire. Trim the ends of the 20-gauge wire with wire cutters and press to secure using flatnose or duckbill pliers **(d)**.

8. Make a "U-shaped bend" in each tail 1" from the end of the wire **(e)**.

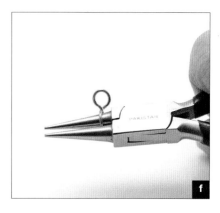

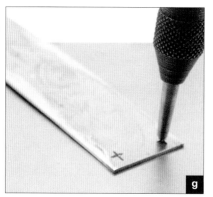

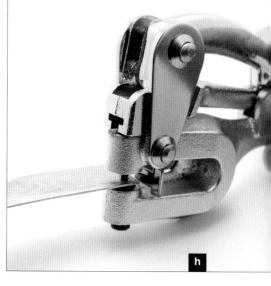

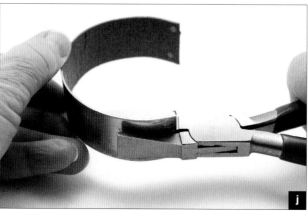

9. Cut the remaining 18-gauge wire into eight 1½" pieces. Form eight reverse Figure-8 links and attach to make a chain **(Techniques, p. 109) (f)**.

10. Use a permanent marker to mark locations for a hole in each corner of the copper strip ³⁄₁₆" from each edge.

11. Make a divot at each mark with a center punch and steel bench block **(g)**.

12. Punch ⅛" holes at each divot **(Techniques, p. 99) (h)**.

13. Apply patina **(Techniques, p. 102-103)**.

14. Remove the copper once it's darkened and wash the surface with dish soap and water. Rinse and dry, then lightly sand the etched surface using a 600-grit sanding stick. Rinse and dry a second time.

15. Using 240-grit sandpaper, sand the opposite side to make some "tooth" for the adhesive.

16. Apply painter's tape to the etched design to protect it while forming. With the etched side facing in, bend the copper strip around a soup can **(i)**.

17. You will need to manipulate the strip with flatnose or duckbill pliers to assist in making the curve **(j)**.

18. Remove the backing from the copper foil and crumple it lightly. (Avoid making a ball, the intention is to keep the foil flat and create ripples.) Using only your fingers, apply light pressure to flatten the foil **(k)**.

19. Apply three lines of cyanoacrylate adhesive to the strip on the roughed-up side **(l)**.

20. Carefully press the prepared foil onto the copper strip to secure **(m)**.

21. When first application of adhesive is dry, trim the excess foil with metal shears.

22. Wrap flatnose or duckbill pliers with one layer of painter's tape. Working along one edge at a time, carefully dab adhesive between the foil and copper, then squeeze with flatnose or duckbill pliers. When dry, repeat on the other edge. Flatten the foil evenly across the strip to compress the ripples.

TIP **It is best to apply the adhesive sparingly, and on one edge at a time to avoid excess and/or sticking the pieces to your fingers.**

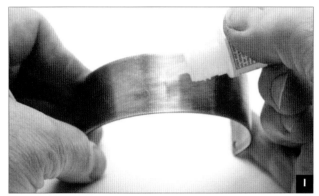

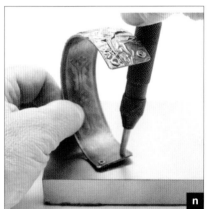
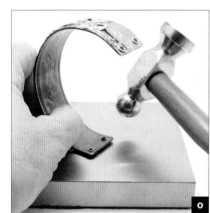

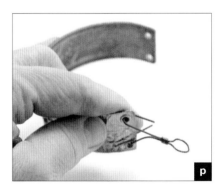
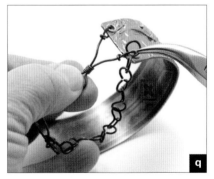

23. When the adhesive is completely dry, use the 360-grit sanding stick to smooth the edges. Then use a 600-grit sanding stick for a finer finish.

24. Punch through the foil at the clasp attachment holes with a 1.8 mm hole punch.

25. Install the eyelets by using the center punch on a steel bench block to start to flare **(n)**.

26. Gently hammer to complete flaring using the chasing hammer **(Techniques, p. 101) (o)**.

27. To secure the wire clasp components to either side of the cuff, thread the "U" shaped wires through the eyelets on the strip. Make a wrapped loop with the tail. Trim and tuck the ends **(p)**.

28. Secure the keeper chain to the wrapped loop on one side of the clasp. Repeat to attach the opposite end of the chain to the other end of the bracelet **(q)**.

29. Adjust the bracelet as necessary and seal with a spray sealant.

Copper and Chain Bracelet

Bring together etched or embossed copper and antiqued copper chain to create a bangle bracelet in a boho style. Totally cold connected, the keeper is formed using wire, then riveted to the last copper square.

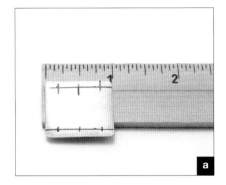

a

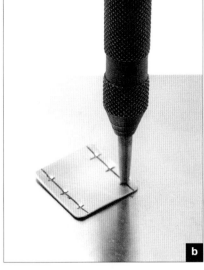

b

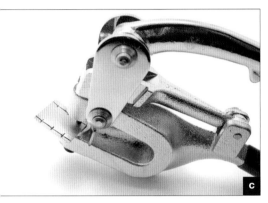

c

d

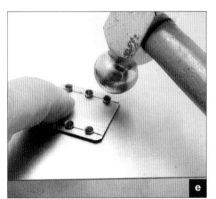

e

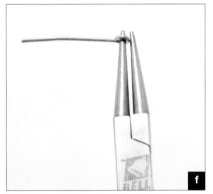

f

materials

- 1" x 4" 22-gauge copper, etched or embossed sheet
- 14" antiqued copper chain
- **19** 18-gauge 8mm copper jump rings
- **18** 1/8" copper eyelets
- 1½" 16-gauge copper wire
- **2** 1/16" x 1/4" flat-head copper rivets

tools

- BASIC TOOL KIT **PG.8**
- 1/8" drill bit
- 1/8" Power punch
- Bentnose pliers
- Brass brush
- Flat needle file
- Liver of sulfur and glass container

47

1. Cut the copper strip into four 1" x 1" pieces using metal shears.

2. Round the edges using a metal file. Smooth with a 360-grit sanding stick **(Techniques, p. 100).**

3. Using the ruler and permanent marker, draw a line 1/8" from both edges on two squares; then mark points at 3/16", 1/2", and 13/16"**(a)**.

4. Using the ruler and permanent marker, draw a line 1/8" from one edge on two squares; then mark points at 3/16", 1/2", and 13/16 ".

5. Make a divot using the center punch at all marked points **(b)**.

6. Punch 1/8" divots **(Techniques, p. 99) (c)**.

7. Set the eyelets by installing the eyelet with the finished side on the etched or embossed face. Lay the pieces etched side down one at a time on the steel bench block and use a center punch to begin to flare the eyelet **(d)**.

8. Finish setting the eyelets by gently tapping the flare using the chasing hammer **(Techniques, p. 101) (e)**.

9. For the closure eye, grasp one end of the 16-gauge wire and make a 2mm plain loop with roundnose pliers **(f)**.

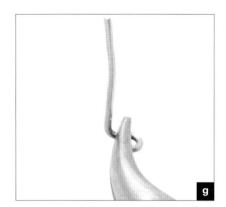

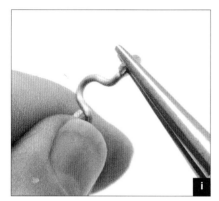

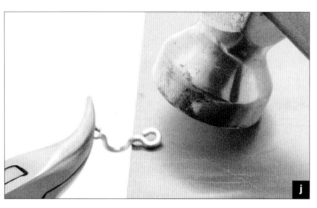

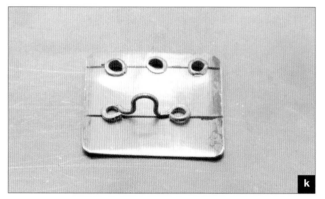

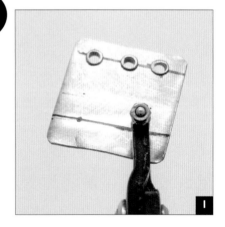

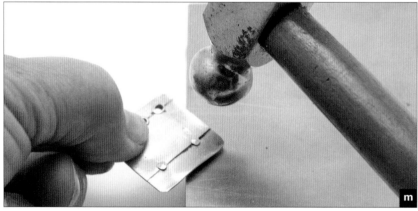

10. Bend the tail at a 90-degree angle using bentnose pliers **(g)**.

11. Use roundnose pliers to make a 6mm "U" bend and then bend the tail outward at 90 degrees in the same plane as the first 90-degree bend **(h)**.

12. Finish off the tail by making a 2mm plain loop using roundnose pliers **(i)**.

13. Flatten the loops on a steel bench block with a chasing hammer **(j)**.

14. Adjust the loops if necessary.

15. Using one of the squares with three punched holes, measure ¼" from the opposite edge and draw a line with the permanent marker. Center the closure loop on the line and mark the location of the plain loops **(k)**.

16. Make a divot at each mark using the center punch; punch the holes using a 1.8mm hole punch **(l)**.

17. Rivet the closure loop to the square **(Techniques, p. 101) (m)**.

18. On the other square with the three punched holes, measure ¼" from the edge opposite the eyelets and draw a line. Mark the centerline and mark ⅛" from the center on both sides.

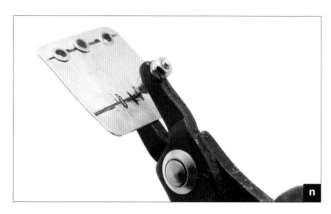

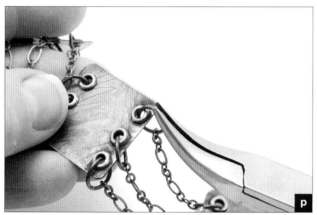

19. Using a 1.8mm hole punch, punch along the line to create a slot for the closure loop to slide through **(n)**.

20. File the slot smooth using a flat needle file **(o)**.

21. Apply patina **(Techniques, p. 102-103)**.

22. Remove the copper and wash the surface with dish soap and water. Rinse and dry the squares, then lightly sand the surfaces using a 600-grit sanding stick. Rinse and dry the squares a second time.

23. Cut 10 1¼" pieces of antique copper chain. Using bentnose pliers, attach nine pieces of the chain between the copper squares using jump rings **(Techniques, p. 109) (p)**.

24. Attach the last piece of chain to the middle jump ring on the square with the slot. Attach the lobster claw clasp to the opposite end with a jump ring **(q)**.

25. This is how the clasp will look when the bracelet is closed **(r)**.

Stackable Embellished Bracelets

50

This project will show you how to transform copper wire into beautiful customizable bangle bracelets. You can mix the type and gauge of wire. You can flatten it, hammer it, and/or add beads, ribbon, and charms.

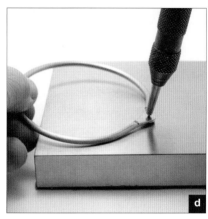

materials

- 9" 8-gauge copper wire
- 24" 16-gauge dark annealed steel wire
- $\frac{1}{16}$" x $\frac{5}{16}$"-gauge rivets

tools

- BASIC TOOL KIT PG.8
- 12mm mandrel
- Ball-peen hammer
- Bentnose pliers
- Cyanoacrylate adhesive
- Jeweler's saw with #1 blade
- Soup can
- Wire cutters

Bracelet Chart

Circumference	Diameter	Size	Wire Length
7.5"	2.375"	Small	8"
8.25"	2.675"	Medium	8¾"
8.5"	2.750"	Large	9"

1. Use a jeweler's saw with a #1 blade to cut a piece of 8-gauge wire to the length needed for the bracelet you wish to make **(a)**. Refer to the bracelet chart above to determine the length needed. *(Please note these are approximate.)* If necessary, clean the wire using a 600-grit sanding stick **(Techniques, p. 100)**.

2. Mark ⅜" from either end of your wire using a permanent marker.

3. With the flat face of your ball-peen hammer, flatten the wire up to the mark. This is where you will punch a hole for the rivet. After hammering, file the ends with a metal file. (You will smooth them further after riveting.) **(b)**

4. Position the wire so the hammered ends are horizontal. Bend your wire around a soup can to begin making the bangle shape **(c)**.

TIP Using a soup can will not allow you to complete the bend, it will only begin the shape. Complete the bend with flatnose or duckbill pliers, working on both ends until they are rounded and meet when you squeeze the bracelet together.

5. Once you've reached your desired diameter, use the permanent marker to mark the location of one hole. Make a divot using a center punch **(d)**.

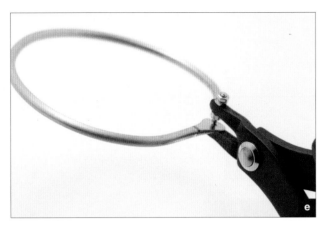

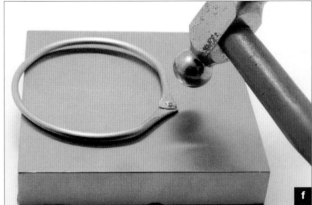

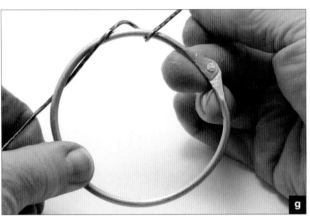

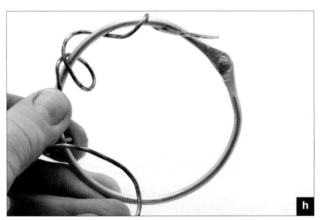

6. Make a hole at the divot using a 1.8mm hole punch **(Techniques, p. 99) (e)**.

7. Squeeze the ends together, and mark the other end through the hole in the first end with your permanent marker. Make a divot using the center punch and then punch a 1.8mm hole.

8. Set a rivet at the join **(Techniques, p. 101) (f)**.

9. Using a metal file, clean up the connection. Use a 360-grit sanding stick to smooth and remove any burrs. Then use a 600-grit sanding stick to refine the connection point.

10. Hammer a 24" length of iron wire with the ball-peen hammer on a steel bench block to add texture. Hammer both ends to flatten. Clean the wire with a 600-grit sanding stick.

TIP **To determine the approximate amount of wire needed to wrap the bangle, double the circumference and add 8".**

11. Wrap one flattened end around the bracelet near the join **(g)**.

12. Continue to randomly wrap the wire around the bracelet **(h)**.

13. Finish the opposite end by wrapping the same as you began. Wrap both ends of the steel wire tightly around the copper and tuck in the ends with bentnose pliers **(i)**.

14. Seal the bracelet with a spray sealant.

Ribbon Wrapped Bracelet

You can dress up the bangle to reflect your personal style by wrapping it with your choice of ribbon or cord. The ribbon and cord are secured by wrapping them with 18-gauge wire.

materials

- 9" 8-gauge copper wire
- 24" 18-gauge copper wire
- $^1/_{16}$" x $^5/_{16}$" copper rivet
- 36" ribbon
- 36" cord

tools

- BASIC TOOL KIT PG.8
- Bentnose pliers

Make a bracelet up to step 9 of the Stackable Embellished Bracelets, then continue as follows:

15. Cut a 24" piece of 18-gauge copper wire, a 36" piece of ribbon, and a 36" piece of cord.

16. Tie the ribbon and cord onto the copper bracelet. Wrap the ribbon around the entire bracelet **(a)**.

17. Tie off the ribbon end. Wrap the cord around the bracelet and tie it off **(b)**.

18. Make four or five wraps with the wire near the tied-off ribbon and cord. Secure with bentnose pliers. Continue to wrap the wire around the bracelet and then terminate it by making four or five wraps **(c)**.

19. To further secure the ribbon ends, place a small dot of cyanoacrylate adhesive on the finished end.

Jump Ring Wrapped Bangle

This project lends itself to adding jump rings for an interesting twist. You can make your own jump rings or purchase them in different colors for a funky twist.

materials
- 9" 8-gauge copper wire
- 44" 14-gauge copper wire (or **21** 14-gauge 12mm purchased jump rings)
- $^1/_{16}$" x $^5/_{16}$" copper rivet

tools
- BASIC TOOL KIT **PG.8**
- 12mm mandrel

Make a bracelet up to step 7 of Stackable Embellished Bracelets, then continue as follows:

20. Using the 1.8mm hole punch, make holes $^3/_{16}$" from the rivet hole on each end of the 8-gauge wire **(a)**.

21. Wrap a 14-gauge wire around a 12mm mandrel in order to make 21 jump rings **(b)**.

22. Remove the jump rings from the mandrel and cut them with flush cutters **(Techniques, p. 109) (c)**. Use a metal file to smooth the ends of the rings.

23. Connect the jump rings into a chain and slide each ring onto the bracelet **(d)**.

24. Set the rivet. **(Techniques, p. 101) (e)**.

25. Using a metal file, clean up the connection. Use a 360-grit sanding stick to make the connection point smooth. Then use a 600-grit sanding stick for a finer finish **(Techniques, p. 100)**.

26. Open an end jump ring and thread it through a hole next to the rivet. Repeat using the opposite end of the chain and remaining hole on the other side of the rivet **(f)**.

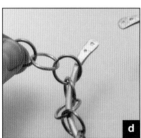

necklaces

Heart-in-Hands Pendant

Several pieces of mixed metals will come together to form a beautiful pendant that is pierced and texturized, featuring a hidden cold connected bail. You will save the heart shape that you sawed from the bronze middle section, and use it as a charm that hangs from the bottom, echoing your cut out in the middle section.

Skills
drilling
making spectacle links
piercing
riveting
texturizing

56

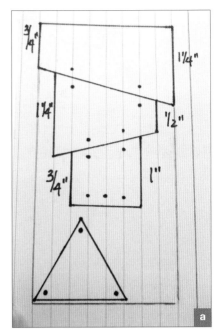

Heart pattern 100%

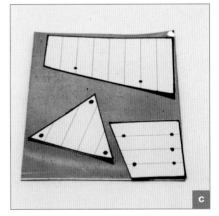

materials

- 2" x 4" 24-gauge copper sheet
- 1½" x 1½" 24-gauge bronze sheet
- 2 copper hand charms
- 3 ¹⁄₁₆" x ⁵⁄₁₆" copper rivets
- 10½" 16-gauge copper wire
- Leather or multi-strand neckwire

tools

- BASIC TOOL KIT **PG.8**
- 4mm mandrel
- #52 drill bit
- Beeswax (or cut lube)
- 2 pairs bentnose pliers
- Cross-peen hammer
- Index card with lines
- Jeweler's saw with #1 blade
- Nail set (assortment)
- Pin vise (or flex shaft)
- Rawhide mallet
- Spring clamp

57

1. To make the pattern, draw a 2" x 4" rectangle on a lined index card. Measure 1¼" down the right and ¾" down the left. Draw a line to connect. Starting one line in on either side, measure ½" down on the right and 1¼" down on the left, draw a line to connect. Starting one line in on either side, measure 1" down on the right and ¾" down on the left, draw a line to connect. Using a 1¼" triangle pattern, draw one triangle. Using the lines on the index card, mark the hanging holes. These marks should be ⅛" from the edges **(a)**.

2. Cut out the card patterns with scissors. Using a 1.8mm hole punch, punch the hole locations on the paper patterns **(Techniques, p. 99) (b)**.
3. Trace the top, bottom, and triangle patterns onto the copper sheet **(c)**.
4. Trace the middle pattern onto the bronze sheet, and draw an offset heart with a permanent marker **(d)**.
5. Cut out all pieces (except the heart) with metal shears **(Techniques, p. 98) (e)**.

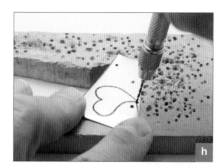

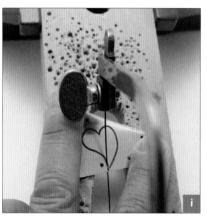

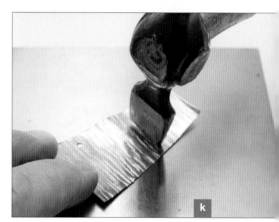

6. Make a divot using a center punch at all hanging hole locations **(f)**.

7. Punch all hanging holes using the 1.8mm hole punch **(g)**.

8. Make a divot at the point of the heart using the #52 drill bit in the pin vise (or flex shaft). Drill a hole at the divot **(Techniques, p. 98) (h)**.

9. Thread the jeweler's saw blade through the hole and tighten the blade **(Techniques, p. 104)**. Apply beeswax (or cut lube) to the blade. Using your bench pin for support, carefully pierce the heart shape. Save the cut out heart **(i)**.

10. File and sand the edges of the heart cut out, as well as the interior of the bronze piece where the heart shape was pierced **(Techniques, p. 100)**.

11. Punch a hanging hole in the heart using a 1.8mm hole punch.

12. To make the hidden bail, use the 1¼" triangle of copper. Using a center punch, make a divot at marks for the rivets. Using a 1.8mm hole punch, make holes at the divots and set aside **(j)**.

13. Texturize the top piece of copper with a cross-peen hammer **(Techniques, p. 98) (k)**.

14. Use the nail sets on the bottom piece of copper and on the hidden bail to add texture **(l)**.

TIP **The pieces will arc after texturizing. You will need to flatten them using a rawhide mallet on the steel bench block.**

15. File all edges with a metal file, paying special attention to round off the corners. Use a 600-grit sanding stick to refine the edges **(Techniques, p. 100)**.

16. Using a 4mm mandrel, center the triangle on the mandrel and bend the piece around it **(m)**.

17. Make two 90-degree bends in the triangle on either side of the bend using flatnose or duckbill pliers **(n)**. Make sure the triangle fits on the top piece.

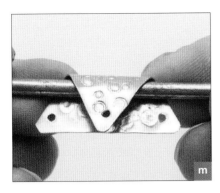

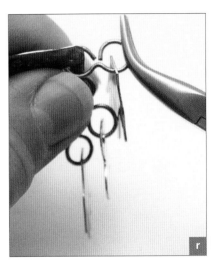

18. Mark the center line on the backside of the top piece, as well as the center line on the bail.

19. Using a spring clamp, secure the bail to the top piece. The clamp will also serve as a handle while riveting **(o)**.

20. Make one hole through the top piece with the 1.8mm hole punch, using a hole in the triangle as a guide **(p)**.

21. Clamp the ³⁄₃₂" nail set in your bench vise, cup side facing up. This will serve as a holder for the rivet head.

22. Insert one rivet through the holes, making sure the round head is on the front side. Trim the rivet with wire cutters to approximately ¹⁄₁₆" and file flat with a metal file. Using the ball face of the chasing hammer, lightly hammer the cut end of the rivet to flatten it out. **(Techniques, p. 101) (q)**.

23. Repeat steps 20–22 for remaining two rivets.

TIP **Remember to only punch one hole at a time; this will alleviate any alignment problems.**

24. Make a spectacle link **(Techniques, p. 106).**

25. To assemble the pendant, use two pairs of bentnose pliers to attach the seven spectacle links between the components. Attach the cut-out heart to the center of the bottom piece, and the hand charms to either side **(r)**.

26. Make a multi-strand neck wire **(Techniques, p. 110)** or use a leather cord to hold the pendant.

Copper Washer Necklace

This necklace is simple, but elegant. Texturized copper washers combine with jump rings and reverse Figure-8 links to create a lightweight and flowing necklace. Since the jump rings and links are not soldered closed, it is important to use reverse Figure-8 links, as washers are thin enough they may slip through even the tightest closed ring.

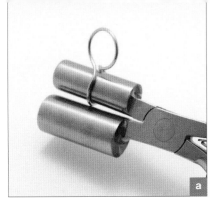

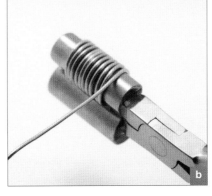

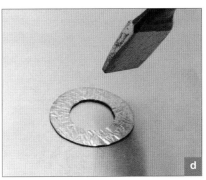

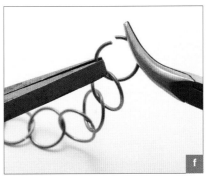

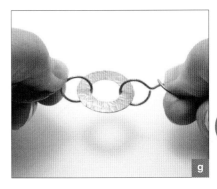

1. Cut 10 3¼" pieces of 16-gauge wire with flush cutters. File the ends flat with a metal file **(Techniques, p. 100)**.

2. Wrap each of the 3¼" pieces of wire around the mandrel pliers, completing a reverse Figure-8 link. **(a)**. Repeat this step, making a total of 10 reverse Figure-8 links **(Techniques, p. 109)**.

3. Use the remaining wire to make 36 jump rings **(Techniques, p. 109) (b)**.

4. Cut the rings using flush cutters **(c)**.

5. Hammer the rings with the rawhide mallet on a bench block to work-harden them.

6. Using a cross-peen hammer and a bench block, apply texture to the copper washers on both sides **(d)**.

7. Flatten them if necessary using the rawhide mallet. Smooth the edges of the washers first with the metal file, then finish with a 600-grit sanding stick **(Techniques, p. 100) (e)**.

8. To assemble the jump rings into a chain, use flatnose pliers and bentnose pliers to grab on either side of the join. Pull one side toward you and push the other away **(Techniques, p. 109) (f)**. Insert a ring and close it. Repeat to attach all of the jump rings.

9. Using the same technique as for the jump rings, open one side at a time on the reverse Figure-8 links and slide on a copper washer. Continue to link the washers onto the reverse Figure-8 links **(g)**.

10. Complete your necklace by attaching the last reverse Figure-8 link on either side to the jump ring chain you made in step 8 **(h)**.

TIP **Using the same size components as called for in the materials section will result in a necklace 18" long. This will easily slip over your head.**

Ellipse Necklace

This project will show you how to combine a copper sheet and copper wire into a beautiful necklace. While I will reference the salt and ammonia patina method for adding some color, you may choose to leave it unfinished, allowing it to age gracefully. If you love the shiny copper finish, clean it up after assembly and apply a spray sealant.

Skills
applying patina
cutting with shears
filing & sanding
making a clasp
making Figure-8 links

**Ellipse patterns
100%**

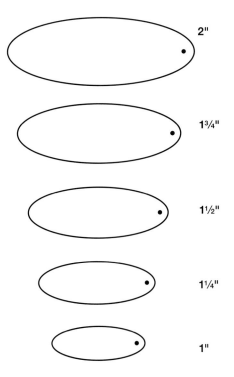

2"

1¾"

1½"

1¼"

1"

materials

- 2½" x 3½" 24-gauge copper sheet (amount determined by design)
- 78" of 16-gauge copper wire

tools

- BASIC TOOL KIT **PG.8**
- 12mm mandrel
- **2** pairs bentnose pliers
- Flush cutters

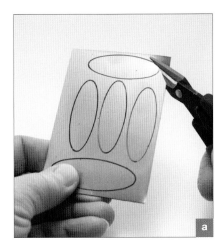

a

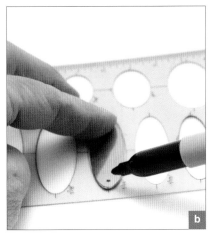

b

c

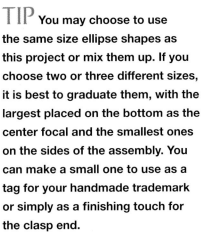

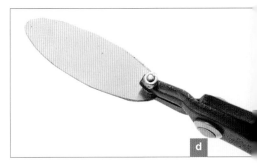

d

TIP **You may choose to use the same size ellipse shapes as this project or mix them up. If you choose two or three different sizes, it is best to graduate them, with the largest placed on the bottom as the center focal and the smallest ones on the sides of the assembly. You can make a small one to use as a tag for your handmade trademark or simply as a finishing touch for the clasp end.**

1. Trace your desired ellipse shapes onto the copper sheet. I will be using one 2" and four 1¾" shapes.

2. Cut out the shapes with metal shears **(Techniques, p. 98) (a)**.

3. Mark the hanging holes with a permanent marker **(b)**.

4. Using a center punch and a bench block, make a divot at each mark **(c)**.

5. Use a 1.8mm hole punch to make holes at the divots **(Techniques, p. 99 (d)**.

6. Lightly file the five pieces. Smooth the edges using a 360-grit sanding stick. Then use a 600-grit sanding stick for a finer finish **(Techniques, p. 100)**. Set aside.

TIP **Making Figure-8 chain links: Each link is ½" long, so for each inch of chain you desire you will need two reverse Figure-8 links. I will base my quantity of links needed for making a 20" long chain. You will need to factor in five additional links to use for attaching your ellipse shapes.**

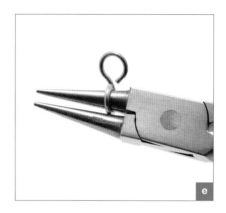

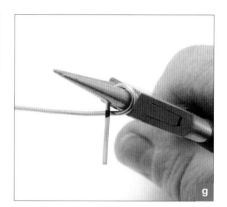

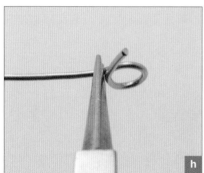

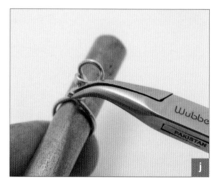

7. Lightly sand the 16-gauge wire with 600-grit sandpaper. Cut 45 pieces of wire 1½" long with flush cutters. File ends flat using a metal file. Using the large end of your roundnose pliers, form opposing plain loops on either end making a reverse Figure-8 link. If necessary, straighten and adjust the loops to make sure they are completely closed and perpendicular to one another **(Techniques, p. 109) (e)**.

8. Assemble two 10" lengths of chain using 40 of the 45 links **(f)**.

9. Cut one piece of 16-gauge wire 3" long and one 3¾" long with flush cutters. File ends flat using a metal file. Mark ½" on one end of the 3" wire. Mark ½" on both ends of the 3¾" wire.

10. Place your roundnose pliers at the ½" mark and form a loop on one end of both wires, bringing the mark to the wire **(g)**.

11. Break the neck of the loops so they are centered on the wire **(h)**.

12. Bend the 3¾" wire above the loop and around the 12mm mandrel; you will now have two ½" **(i)**.

13. Wrap the ½" tails of the 3¾" wire in opposite directions. Trim and tuck the wires **(j)**.

14. To make the hook, flatten the opposite end of the 3¾" wire perpendicular to the loop. Wrap the wire around the mandrel to make a hook shape **(k)**. Wrap the ½" tail; trim and tuck the end. Make a slight outward bend on the flattened part with your roundnose pliers.

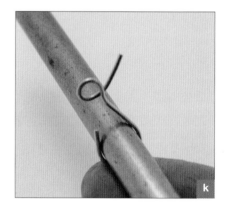

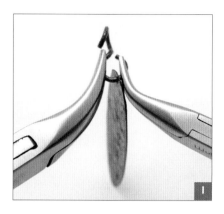

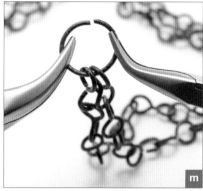

15. Hammer the hook and the large loop using a chasing hammer.

16. With the remaining length of wire, make one 8mm jump ring.

17. Re-sand all of the components with 600-grit sandpaper. This will remove the shiny mill finish and prepare them for the patina.

18. If desired, apply an amonia and salt patina **(Techniques, p.102)**.

19. Attach the remaining five Figure-8 links to the ellipse shapes with two pairs of bentnose pliers **(l)**.

20. Use the 8mm jump ring to connect the two 10" pieces of chain **(m)**.

21. Attach the 2" ellipse shape to the jump ring. Then equally space the remaining ellipse shapes on the chain **(n)**.

22. Attach the clasp pieces to the ends of the chains.

23. Seal the entire piece with a spray sealant.

65

Tumbling

If you find you are creating more metal jewelry and wish to streamline the process of removing mill finish from metals, you may wish to invest in a basic rock tumbler. I find it handy when I have a large number of pieces I wish to prepare to accept patina and I don't have the time (or patience!) to hand sand each piece.

Loading a tumbler with some medium or coarse pyramid shot, water, and your metal is an easy way to prepare a large number of pieces. No need to run the tumbler very long; an hour or two (at the most) is perfect for removing the mill finish. When the mill finish is totally removed from your pieces, remove them from the tumbler, give them a quick wash with plain dish soap, and dry them.

Strap-Set Pendant

I must admit I am a collector of stuff. Sea glass naturally caught my eye, as well as beach stones, shells, bones, old buttons, rust, the list goes on. My goal was to design a way to capture these items whose shape would not necessarily conform to a basic tab setting. This project presents a new twist on tab setting, and works perfect for those fantastic less-than-perfect pieces you wish to showcase in a setting. Using a paper pattern made directly on the piece you wish to capture creates a pattern for the strap setting.

Skills
applying patina
filing & sanding
hole punching
riveting
texturizing

Funky shapes

Sea glass, shell fragments, or a piece of a Coke bottle can be used as focal pieces for a strap-set pendant. Because these shapes are often irregular in form, they do not lend themselves to traditional bezel setting. However, strap setting items like these can result in showing off the treasures in a totally different way.

materials

- 3" x 4" 24-gauge copper sheet
- **3** $^1/_{16}$" x $^5/_{16}$" copper rivets
- **3** 18-gauge 10mm jump rings
- Lobster claw clasp
- 18" chain
- Object to capture

tools

- BASIC TOOL KIT **PG.8**
- Bentnose pliers
- Index cards
- Liver of sulfur (optional)

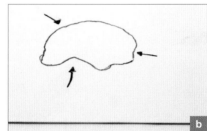

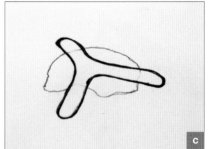

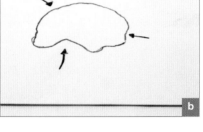

1. Lay the object you will be setting on an index card and trace around it **(a)**.

2. Looking at the drawing, mark arrows to show the best position for straps to hold the object in place **(b)**.

TIP **You will likely need three or more straps to prevent the object from slipping out of the setting.**

3. Draw the straps and extend them beyond the edges of the object **(c)**.

4. If your object is not completely flat, measure its height at the highest point and double check the length of the straps to assure the strap you make will be long enough to reach the copper backing.

5. Cut out your paper pattern strap with scissors. Place your object on another index card and trace around it. Test the paper pattern to make sure it will not only fit over the object, but that you have enough strap left over to bend and insert a rivet to the copper backing. Mark the index card where the tabs will be located **(d)**.

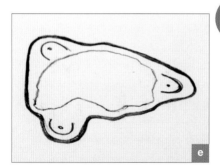
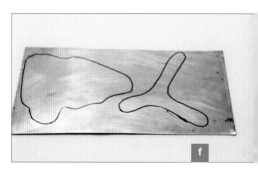

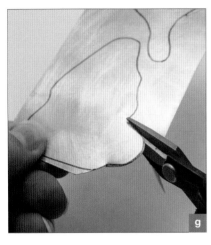

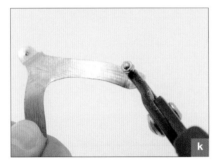

6. After testing the fit of the straps, draw the outline of the shape and straps to make the pattern for the copper back plate. Cut out the pattern with scissors **(e)**.

7. Trace the back plate pattern and strap pattern onto the piece of copper **(f)**.

8. Cut out both patterns using metal shears **(Techniques, p. 98) (g)**.

9. File the edges with a metal file. Use a 360-grit sanding stick to smooth and refine the shapes. Then use a 600-grit sanding stick for a finer finish **(Techniques, p. 100)**.

10. To add texture, sand the surface with 600-grit sandpaper. This will make small scratches in the copper. Do the same on the front side of the strap **(h)**.

11. Align the strap and object on the copper back plate. Using flatnose pliers, bend the tabs perpendicular to the back plate. Manipulate the strap, to conform to the shape of the object **(i)**.

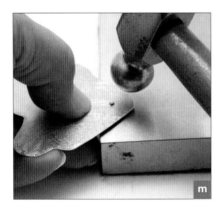

12. Mark the rivet holes on the straps then use a center punch on a steel bench block to make a divot **(j)**.

13. Make a hole at the end of each tab using a 1.8mm hole punch **(Techniques, p. 99) (k)**.

14. Align the strap with the object and copper back plate. Make a hole through the back plate at one of the strap ends with a 1.8mm hole punch **(l)**.

15. Insert one rivet so the flat side is on the front.

16. Trim the rivet with wire cutters to about ¹⁄₁₆" and set it with a chasing

hammer **(Techniques, p. 101) (m)**.

17. Punch and rivet the second and third straps in the same manner.

18. Choose the side from where you wish to hang the pendant and punch a hole ⅛" from the edge of the back plate. Apply patina **(Techniques, p. 102-103)**.

19. Using bentnose pliers and flatnose pliers, thread one jump ring through the hanging hole in the pendant and through the center link of the chain **(n)**.

20. Using both pliers, attach a jump ring and lobster claw to one end of the chain. Attach a jump ring to the other end.

Petals and Vines Choker

Skills
cutting with shears
drilling
hole punching
making Figure-8 links
texturizing

Alexander Calder was an incredibly talented artist, most famous for his mobiles. However, he also produced amazing jewelry. This choker was inspired by a hammered silver and steel wire bracelet he designed. Aluminum and copper petal shapes formed in a bead scoop are in the forefront. Wrapping the necklace with wire imitates vines and adds another dimension to the piece.

materials

- 2½" x 4" 24-gauge copper sheet
- 2½" x 4" 24-gauge aluminum sheet
- 18" 8-gauge copper wire
- 5½" 16-gauge copper wire
- 30" 18-gauge copper wire
- 36" 18-gauge bronze wire

tools

- BASIC TOOL KIT **PG.8**
- #52 drill bit
- Bead scoop
- Electrical tape
- Pin vise (or flex shaft)

Ellipse patterns 100%

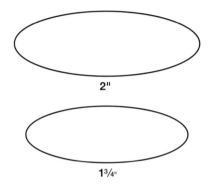
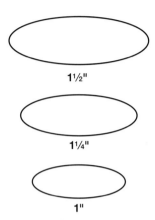

2"

1¾"

1½"

1¼"

1"

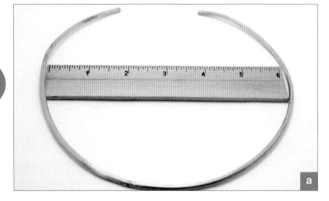
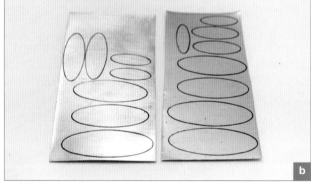
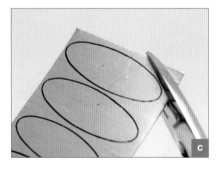

1. Shape the 8-gauge copper wire into a circular shape using your hands. Aim for an inside diameter of approximately 6". Set aside **(a)**.

2. Using the permanent marker, draw 15 petal shapes on the sheet metal using the ellipse pattern as follows: one 2" copper, two 1¾" copper, two 1½" copper, two 1" copper, two 2" aluminum, two 1¾" aluminum, two 1¼" aluminum, and two 1" aluminum **(b)**.

3. Cut out the petal shapes with metal shears **(Techniques. p. 98) (c)**.

4. Lay the shapes on a bench block. Texture each petal with the round head of a chasing hammer **(Techniques, p. 98) (d)**.

5. To add a slight concave to the petal shape, use the ball face of a chasing hammer to sink each petal into a bead scoop **(e)**.

6. File the edges with a metal file. Then use a 360-grit sanding stick for a smoother finish **(Techniques, p. 100)**.

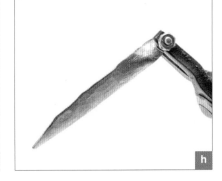

7. Using roundnose pliers, make a vertical bend in the top ¼" of each petal **(f)**.

8. Compress the bend with flatnose pliers, making a closed dart **(g)**.

9. Using a center punch, make a divot on one side of the dart. Punch a hole through both layers of the dart using the 1.8mm hole punch **(Techniques, p. 99) (h)**.

10. Cut 15 1⅜" pieces of 18-gauge copper wire. File all of the ends flat with a metal file.

11. Apply a piece of electrical tape on one jaw of the roundnose pliers at the 4mm measurement. With 18-gauge copper wire, make 15 reverse Figure-8 links with a 4mm loop in each end **(Techniques, p. 109) (i)**.

12. Attach one petal to each reverse Figure-8 link **(j)**.

13. Hammer one end of the 8-gauge neck wire flat using the chasing hammer on a bench block.

14. Slide the petals onto the neck wire, positioning them in a bib formation. Make sure the longest petal is in the center **(k)**.

15. Flatten the opposite end of the neck wire shape **(l)**. File both ends smooth with a metal file and then use a 360-grit sanding stick for a smoother finish.

16. Using a center punch, make a divot centered on each flattened end of the neck wire.

17. Rest one end of the neck wire on the bench pin. Drill a hole into the flat side at the divot using a #52 drill bit in the pin vise (or flex shaft). Repeat for the opposite end of the neck wire **(m)**.

18. Make a mark at the center of the 36" piece of bronze wire.

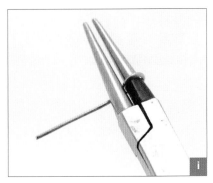

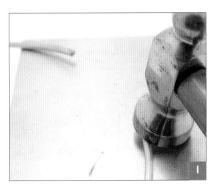

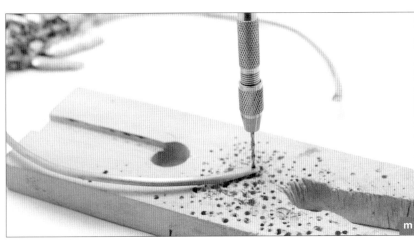

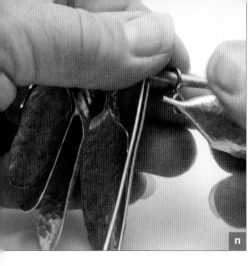

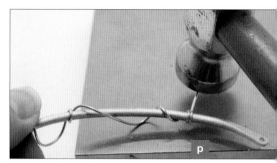

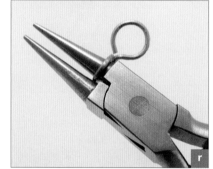
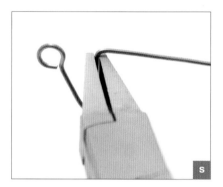
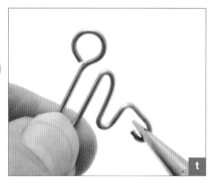

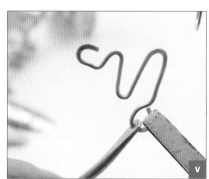

19. Align the center of the bronze wire, on the center of the neck wire, and begin wrapping it around the 8-gauge wire, capturing the petals as you continue **(n)**. Space the petals evenly on the neck wire.

20. Once the petals are captured, manipulate the wire to create a "vine-like effect," continuing toward the flattened ends **(o)**.

21. Terminate the bronze wire on each end by making three tight wraps, and trim the wire to ½" with wire cutters. Flatten the ½" tail using the chasing hammer on a steel bench block **(p)**.

22. File the ends, then press the flattened end snug against the neck wire using flatnose pliers **(q)**.

23. Cut the 16-gauge copper wire into one 3½" piece and one 2" piece. Make a reverse Figure-8 link with a 6mm loop on one end and an 8mm loop on the opposite end of the 2" piece using roundnose pliers **(Techniques, p. 109) (r)**.

24. Make a 6mm loop on one end of the 3½" wire, and bend the tail at a 90-degree angle to the loop. Using flatnose pliers, bend the wire at ⅝" from the loop, then at ⅝" again in the opposite direction, then at ½", then ¼" **(s)**.

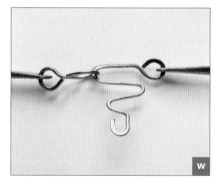

25. Make an inward-facing U-bend using roundnose pliers at ⅛" **(t)**.

26. Flatten the zig-zag piece using a chasing hammer on a steel bench block **(u)**.

27. Attach the clasp components to the 6mm loop of the reverse Figure-8 link **(v, w)**.

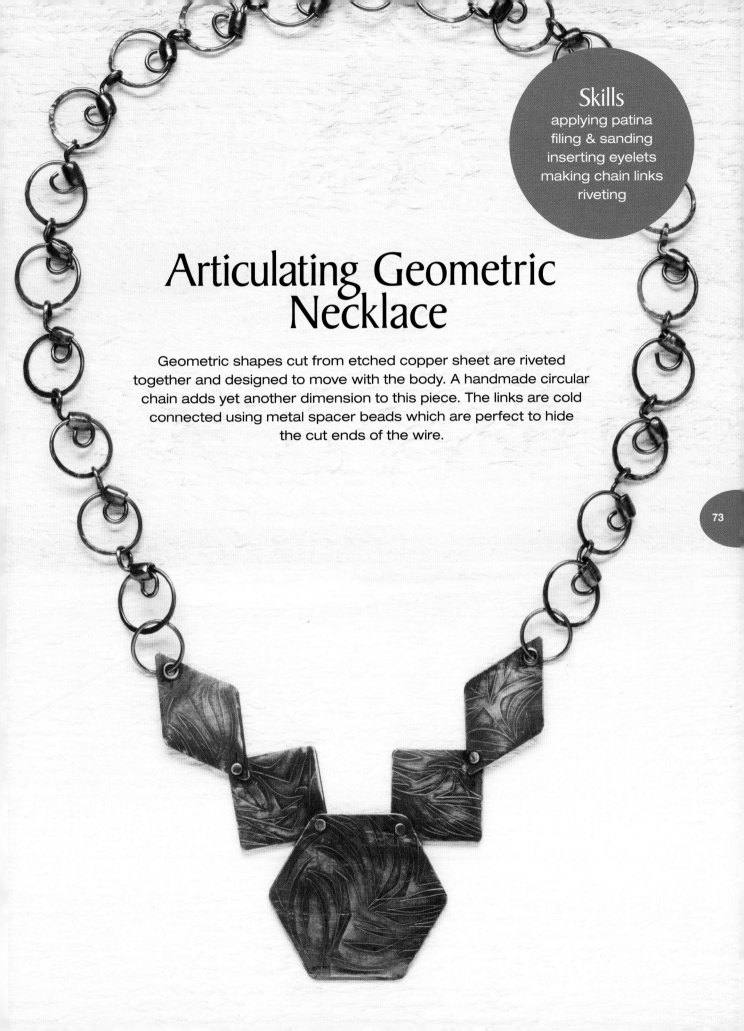

Skills
applying patina
filing & sanding
inserting eyelets
making chain links
riveting

Articulating Geometric Necklace

Geometric shapes cut from etched copper sheet are riveted together and designed to move with the body. A handmade circular chain adds yet another dimension to this piece. The links are cold connected using metal spacer beads which are perfect to hide the cut ends of the wire.

**Geometric patterns
100%**

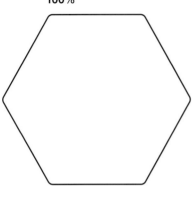

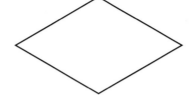

materials

- 6" x 6" 22-gauge etched copper sheet
- **20** 7mm copper spacer beads with 3mm hole
- **4** ¹⁄₁₆" x ⁵⁄₁₆" flat-head copper rivets
- 84" piece 16-gauge copper wire
- **2** ¹⁄₈" eyelets

tools

- BASIC TOOL KIT
- ¹⁄₈" drill bit (or power punch)
- 12mm mandrel
- Liver of sulfur
- Nail sets (assortment)
- Pin vise (or flex shaft) (optional)

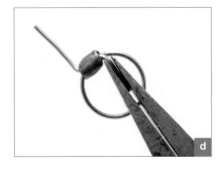

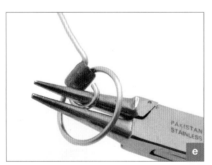

The Chain

1. Clean the 16-gauge wire with 600-grit sandpaper. Cut 20 pieces of wire 3½" long. File all of the ends flat with a metal file **(Techniques, p. 100).**

2. Make a mark ¾" from one end and a mark ½" from the opposite end of each 3½" piece of 16-gauge wire.

3. Center the wire on the 12mm mandrel and bend it around, overlapping the tails **(a).**

4. Remove the wire from the mandrel. Slide a spacer bead over one tail, then the other. Hold the spacer bead in the center **(b).**

5. Using flatnose pliers, bend the wire vertically at the ¾" mark **(c).**

6. Bend the inside tail down at the ½" mark **(d).**

7. Grasp the inside tail with roundnose pliers and make an upward-facing half-loop to capture the spacer bead **(e).**

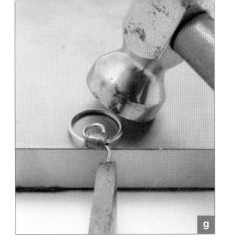

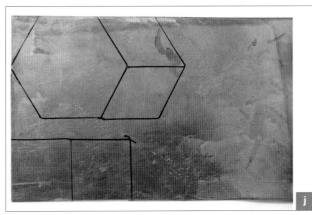

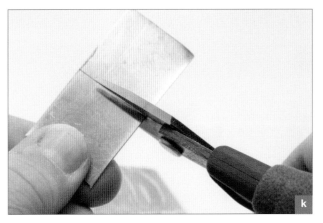

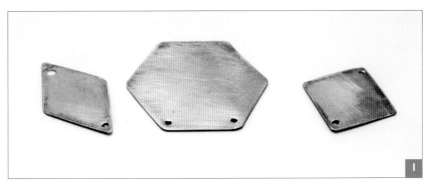

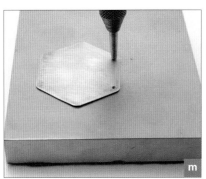

8. Flatten the end of the ¾" bent wire on a steel bench blockwith a chasing hammer. File the end with a metal file, if necessary **(f)**.

9. Lightly hammer the bottom section of the chain link with a chasing hammer **(g)**.

10. Using roundnose pliers, make a bend in the wire towards you to make a plain loop **(h)**.

11. Following steps 3–10, complete the remaining 19 links. Assemble two 10-link chains by attaching the upper plain loop of one link to the larger loop of another **(i)**.

12. With the remaining 16-gauge wire, make three 12mm jump rings **(Techniques, p. 109)**.

The Pendant

13. Using 240-grit sandpaper, sand the back of the pre-made etched or patterned copper sheet **(Techniques, p. 100)**.

14. Trace patterns (found at the beginning of this project) on the backside of the copper sheet using a permanent marker **(j)**.

15. Carefully cut out the shapes using metal shears **(Techniques, p. 98) (k)**.

16. File all the corners and edges with a metal file. Follow with a 360-grit sanding stick to smooth. Then use a 600-grit sanding stick for a finer finish.

17. Using a permanent marker, mark two rivet points ⅛" from the corners on one side of the hexagon.

18. Mark one rivet point ⅛" from a corner of the square shape. Make a second rivet point in the opposite corner of the same square shape. Repeat on the second square shape.

19. Mark a rivet point ⅛" from one corner of both diamond shapes.

20. Mark ⅜" on the other end of each diamond shape. This is where the eyelets will be installed.

21. Using a center punch and a bench block, make divots at all marks **(l)**.

22. Punch a hole in all divots located at the ⅛" mark with a 1.8mm hole punch **(Techniques, p. 99) (m)**.

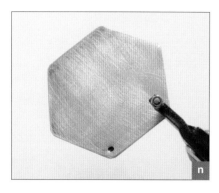

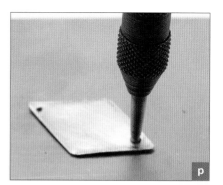

23. Use a ⅛" hole punch or a ⅛" drill bit in a pin vise (or flex shaft) to make a hole for an eyelet at one end of each of the diamond shapes **(n, o)**.

24. Insert the eyelet through the diamond with the finished side on the etched face. Lay the piece etched-side down on the steel bench block and use a center punch to begin to flare the eyelet **(p)**.

25. Finish setting the eyelet by gently tapping the flare using the chasing hammer **(Techniques, p. 100) (q)**. Repeat for the second diamond.

26. Prepare your spacers by cutting six ¼" wide x 3" long pieces of card stock. Fold strips in half and punch a hole on the folded end with the 1.8mm hole punch. Carefully cut a slit to the punched hole using scissors **(r)**.

27. Insert a rivet through the hexagon shape, with the head of the rivet against the etched surface. Then place the paper spacer on the shank, followed by the square shape **(s)**.

28. Set the rivet using a chasing hammer **(Techniques, p. 101) (t)**.

29. Lightly hammer the back of the rivet using a ³⁄₃₂" nail set and the chasing hammer.

30. Remove the paper spacer. Repeat the process with the remaining three rivets.

31. Assemble the necklace by connecting 12mm jump rings through the eyelets and the chain **(u)**.

32. Bring the ends of the chains together using the third 12mm jump ring **(v)**.

33. Apply patina **(Techniques, p. 102-103)**.

34. Remove the necklace and wash the surface with dish soap and water. Rinse and dry the necklace, then lightly sand it using a 600-grit sanding stick. Rinse and dry a second time.

35. Seal the necklace with spray sealant.

Copper Spoon Necklace

Skills
applying patina
dapping
making a clasp
riveting
texturizing

Let your imagination run when it comes to embellishing this necklace. A simple riveted connection allows the necklace to hinge, adding an interesting detail for the eye as well as comfort for the wearer. You will use metal shears to cut copper discs and since the design is a bit edgy, there is no reason for them to be perfect. A dapping block is used to make the discs concave. As you hammer the discs the wire will flatten, creating a secure cold connection. A liver of sulfer patina is applied, and then the pieces are sealed with a spray sealant.

Circle patterns
100%

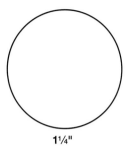

1¼"

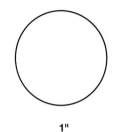

1"

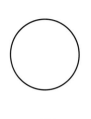

¾"

materials

- 2½"x 4" 24-gauge copper sheet
- 18" 8-gauge copper wire
- 62" 16-gauge copper wire
- 12-gauge wire for mandrel
- 2 ¹⁄₁₆" x ⁵⁄₁₆" flat-head copper rivets
- **6** Beads of your choice
- **8** Copper spacer beads

tools

- BASIC TOOL KIT **PG.8**
- 28-29 oz. metal can
- Index card
- Jeweler's saw with #1 blade
- Liver of sulfur with glass container
- Nail set (assortment)
- Necklace mandrel (or bench block)
- Steel dapping block
- Tubing cutter

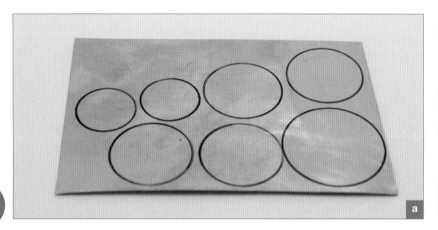

a

78

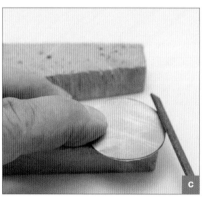

b

c

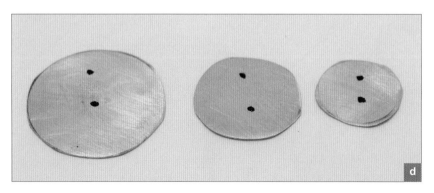

d

1. Lightly sand the copper sheet with 600-grit sandpaper.

2. Using the circle patterns above and a permanent marker, trace the following sized discs on the copper: one 1¼", four 1", and two ¾" **(a)**.

3. Cut out the circles using metal shears; they don't need to be perfect **(Techniques, p. 98) (b)**.

4. File the edges using a metal file **(Techniques, p. 100) (c)**.

5. Using a permanent marker and ruler, mark the locations for punching. On the 1¼" and 1" discs, mark ¼" and ⁵⁄₈" off one edge. On the ¾" discs, mark ¼" and ½" off one edge **(d)**.

6. Make a divot at each mark using a center punch on a steel bench block **(e)**.

7. Punch holes at each divot with a 1.8 mm hole punch **(Techniques, p. 99) (f)**.

8. Clean the 16-gauge copper wire using 600-grit sandpaper. Cut nine pieces 6" long using wire cutters.

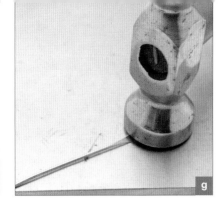

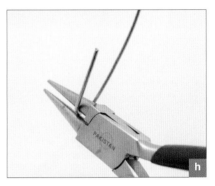
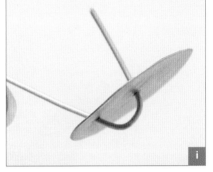
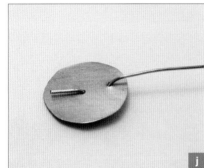

9. File the ends flat with a metal file.

10. Using the chasing hammer, flatten one end on two pieces to resemble a paddle. File the hammered paddle ends smooth. Set aside **(g)**.

11. Using roundnose pliers, bend a shallow 'U' approximately 1" from one end of a plain wire **(h)**.

12. Thread the wire ends through the holes in one of the copper discs and adjust the slack. Press the wire flat against the disc **(i)**.

13. Trim the short end, if needed, so that it does not extend beyond the disc **(j)**.

14. Lay the disc in the large depression of the dapping block. With the ball end of the chasing hammer, begin to hammer the disc including the short end of the wire **(Techniques, p. 98)**. This action will add depth and dimension to the disc as well as flatten out the wire, securing it onto the disc. Avoid hammering the wire as it exits the top of the circle **(k)**.

15. Repeat for the remaining discs. Smooth the edges again, if necessary, with a 360-grit sanding stick. Set them aside.

16. Clean the 8-gauge wire with 600-grit sandpaper.

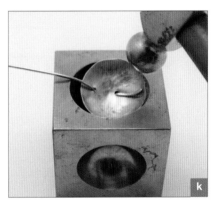
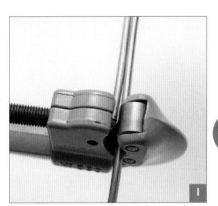

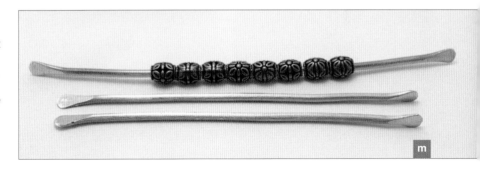

17. Measure 5½" on the 8-gauge wire, and cut at the mark using a tubing cutter or a jeweler's saw with a #1 blade.

18. Using the first 5½" wire as a guide, cut a second 8-gauge wire wire with a tubing cutter or a jeweler's saw and #1 blade **(l)**.

19. Measure a third length of 7" and cut. Slide the eight spacer beads on the 7" wire.

TIP **This measurement can be adjusted as necessary to make the necklace longer if desired.**

20. Using a steel bench block and a ball-peen hammer, flatten both ends of the 7" wire in opposite places. Flatten the ends of the 5½" wires in opposite places **(m)**.

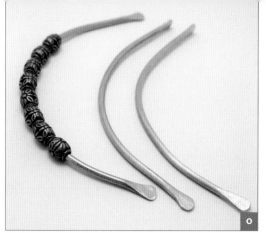

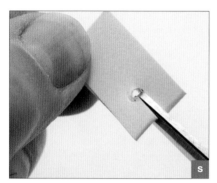

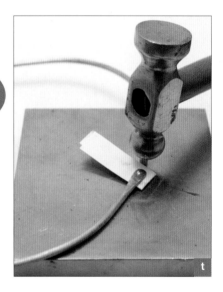

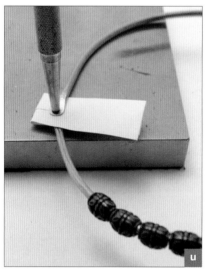

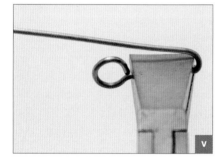

31. Cut a 4" length of 16-gauge wire, and make a 7mm plain loop on one end. Using flatnose pliers, make a bend at ¾" above the loop **(v)**.

32. Make a second bend at ¾" with round nose pliers, then a third bend at ½". Make a 90-degree bend ½" from the previous bend **(w)**.

33. Slide a metal bead onto the wire and flatten the end on a steel bench block with the chasing hammer **(x)**.

34. Grasp the plain loop with flatnose pliers and twist it so it's perpendicular to the hook **(y)**.

35. Cut a piece of 16-gauge wire 2½" long. Make three coils around a piece of 12-gauge wire (serving as the mandrel) **(z)**.

36. Slide the wire off the mandrel and make a 7mm plain loop on the end **(aa)**.

21. File the ends of the wires smooth and round.

22. Use your fingers to begin to curve the wires around the metal soup can **(n)**.

23. Make sure to orient the paddle ends as shown **(o)**.

24. Using the center punch, make a divot ⅛" from the end of each paddle **(p)**.

25. Punch all holes using the 1.8 mm punch **(q)**.

26. Cut two ½" wide x 3" long pieces of card stock or index card. Fold strips in half and punch ½" from the folded end with the 1.8 mm punch **(r)**.

27. Cut a slit to the punched hole using scissors **(s)**.

28. Insert a rivet through one paddle on the 7" wire, then place the paper spacer on the shank. Slide one end of one 5½" wire over the rivet shank. Set the rivet with the chasing hammer **(Techniques, p. 101) (t)**.

29. Finish the back of the rivet by using the 3.2mm nail set to round off the rivet shank **(u)**.

30. Remove the paper spacer and repeat on the opposite end of the 7" wire.

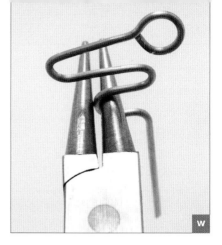

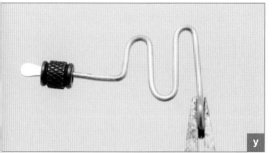

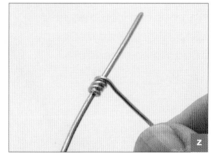

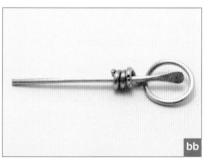

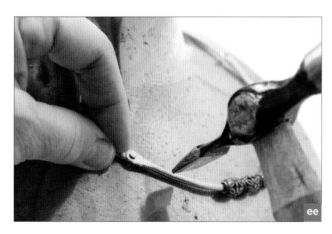

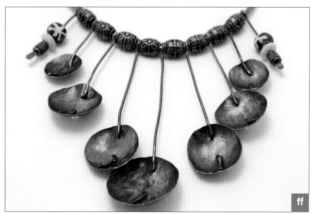

37. Cut a 1½" piece of 16-gauge wire and flatten one end with the chasing hammer. Slide this wire through the coil, flattened end pointing towards the plain loop **(bb)**.

38. Make a 9mm plain loop on the opposite end **(cc)**.

39. Attach the clasp ends to the necklace and place it on the necklace mandrel (or on a bench block) **(dd)**.

40. With the necklace on the mandrel, hammer lightly with a cross-peen hammer to add texture **(Techniques, p. 98) (ee)**.

41. Smooth any burrs made during texturizing using 600-grit sandpaper.

42. Apply patina (**Techniques, p. 102-103**).

43. Thread beads onto the paddle end wires from step 10. Organize the spoon

wires with the largest disc in the center. Trim the center wire to 3" and make a 7mm plain loop. Trim two 1" spoon wires to 2½" and make 7mm plain loops. Trim the ¾" spoon wires to 1¼" and make 7mm loops. Trim the beaded wires to 1" and make 7mm loops. Attach the wires between the spacer beads **(ff)**.

Copper Necklace with Charms

If you like the style of the neck wire part of this project, but want to mix it up a little, you can easily hang your favorite beads from it, instead. Adding handmade copper spacer beads will complete the look.

materials

- 18" 8-gauge copper wire
- 62" 16-gauge copper wire
- 12-gauge wire for mandrel
- 2 $^1/_{16}$" x $^5/_{16}$" flat-head copper rivets
- Beads of your choice
- 8 Copper spacer beads

tools

- BASIC TOOL KIT
- 28-29 oz. metal can
- Index card
- Jeweler's saw with #1 blade (or tubing cutter)
- Liver of sulfur with glass container
- Nail set (assortment)

Make the Copper Spoon Necklace starting with step 16 and continuing through step 40.

44. Measure ¼" on the copper tubing and mark with a permanent marker. Using a jeweler's saw with #1 blade, cut one spacer bead. Continue to measure and cut until you have 12 pieces.

Smooth the edges using a 360-grit sanding stick.

45. Cut the 16-gauge wire into eleven 4" pieces. Use the chasing hammer to flatten one end of each wire to resemble a paddle (See step 10, p. 79.). File the paddle ends smooth.

46. Trim the wires as follows: 1 at 4"; 2 at 3¾", 2 at 3½"; 2 at 2½"; and 2 at 2".

47. Apply patina **(Techniques, p. 102-103).**

48. String your beads onto the paddle end wires.

49. Using roundnose pliers, make 7mm loops in the ends of each beaded wire.

50. Organize the wires on the necklace starting with the 4" wire in the center and end with the 2½" wires at each end.

rings&more

Hammered Copper Ring

This project shows how to make a simple cold connected copper ring by hammering a narrow strip of copper. Hammering with a cross-peen hammer naturally causes the copper to curl and also adds an interesting texture. A simple riveted cold connection seals the seam.

Skills
cutting with shears
filing & sanding
ring sizing
riveting
using a ring mandrel

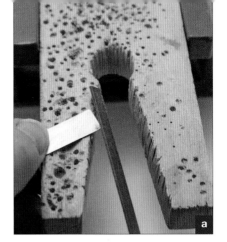

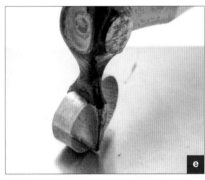

materials

- ³⁄₈" wide strip copper (length determined by ring size)
- 2 ¹⁄₁₆" x ⁵⁄₁₆" flat-head copper rivets

tools

- BASIC TOOL KIT
- Cross-peen hammer
- Bench vise and bench pin
- Steel ring mandrel

Ring sizing Chart

Use the chart below to estimate the length of strip needed to make your size of ring.

Ring Size	Circumference in inches	Strip Length
5	2"	2½"
5½	2"	2½"
6	2¹⁄₁₆"	2⁹⁄₁₆"
6½	2¹⁄₁₆"	2⁹⁄₁₆"
7	2⅛"	2⅝"
7½	2⅛"	2⅝"
8	2¼"	2¾"
8½	2¼"	2¾"
9	2⅜"	2⅞"
9½	2⅜"	2⅞"
10	2½"	3"
10½	2½"	3"

1. Determine the size of the ring you will be making and cut the ³⁄₈" wide copper strip to that length using metal shears **(Techniques p.98)**.

2. Using 600-grit sandpaper, clean the strip; then round off the cut ends with a metal file **(Techniques, p. 100) (a)**.

3. Locate the point for the first rivet ¼" from one end, centered within the strip. Mark with a permanent marker, and then make a divot with the center punch **(b)**.

4. Make a hole at the divot with a 1.8mm hole punch **(Techniques, p.99) (c)**.

5. Lay the strip on the steel bench block with the length positioned vertically. Using the cross-peen hammer, begin hammering the strip horizontally from the end to the center. You will begin to stretch the metal, which will cause it to curl **(d)**.

6. When you get close to the center of the strip, turn it and finish hammering from the other end **(e)**.

TIP **I strongly suggest using a steel ring mandrel to make this project; not only will you maintain the size of the ring, the riveting can be performed directly on the ring mandrel.**

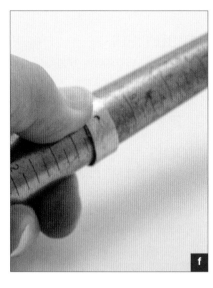

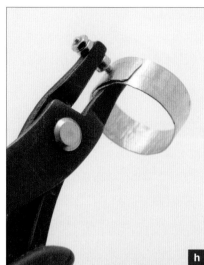

7. Wrap the copper strip around the ring mandrel and center it on the chosen size. (You will end up with an overlap of about ¼" on either side.) Make sure the end with the hole is on the top **(f)**.

8. Using a marker, mark a matching point for the rivet hole **(g)**.

9. Slide the ring off the mandrel and make a hole at the mark with a 1.8mm hole punch, using the first hole as a guide **(h)**.

10. Insert one flat-head rivet from the inside and slide the ring back over the mandrel. With the metal shears, trim the rivet shank to approximately ¹⁄₁₆." Partially set the rivet using a chasing hammer **(Techniques, p. 101) (i)**.

11. With the ring still on the mandrel, locate a second rivet hole. Mark and make a divot with the center punch **(j)**.

12. Remove the ring from the mandrel and make a hole through both layers using a 1.8mm hole punch. Insert the second rivet as in step 10. Slide the ring back onto the mandrel, trim and set. Fully set both rivets.

13. Remove the ring from the mandrel. Sand the surface, edges, and rivet shanks smooth using the 600-grit sanding stick.

14. Seal with a spray sealant.

TIP **Using spray sealant on the copper will help prevent discoloration as the ring rubs against your finger.**

Embellished Ring

This basic ring design lends itself easily to adding a little embellishment.

materials

- ³⁄₈" wide copper strip (length determined by ring size)
- 2 ¹⁄₁₆" x ⁵⁄₁₆" flat-head copper rivets
- 6" each ribbon and cotton cord

tools

- BASIC TOOL KIT PG.8
- Cross-peen hammer
- Bench vise
- Steel ring mandrel
- ⁵⁄₃₂" mandrel (such as a drill bit)

a

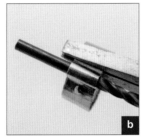

b

c

d

e

f

Follow steps 1–10 for the Hammered Copper Ring and then proceed as follows:

15. Using flatnose pliers, bend the extra length up at a 90-degree angle to the rivet to make a tab **(a)**.

16. Hold ⁵⁄₃₂" mandrel on the ring mandrel on the ring next to the bend and bend the tab over the mandrel. Bend it again at a 90-degree angle next to the mandrel, and squeeze the end flat against the ring shank **(b)**.

17. With the ring still on the mandrel, mark and make a divot with the center punch for the second rivet hole. Remove the ring from the mandrel and make a hole with a 1.8mm hole punch. Insert a second rivet as in steps 11 and 12 of the main project. Slide the ring back on mandrel, trim the rivet with wire cutters, and set it. Fully set both rivets **(c)**.

18. Remove the ring from the mandrel and sand the sides, edges, and rivet shanks with a 600-grit sanding stick.

19. Seal the ring with a spray sealant.

20. Thread the cotton cord and ribbon through the space created with the ⁵⁄₃₂" mandrel. Feed one end through the loop again **(d)**.

21. Tie an overhand knot **(e)**.

22. Using the cotton cord only, tie a square knot to secure by crossing the right side over the left side and pull to tighten. Then cross the left side over the right side, pull to tighten **(f)**. Trim the ends as desired.

Curly Top Ring

The Curly Top Ring is comprised of patterned brass and etched copper; using a different approach to cold connecting. The ring shank is threaded through pierced slots in the copper and brass squares. Slicing the brass thinly causes the pieces to curl; and in turn, those curls are the cold connection holding the ring together.

Skills
dapping
drilling
filing & sanding
piercing
riveting

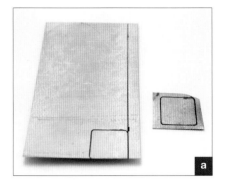

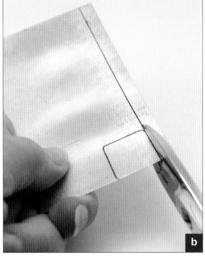

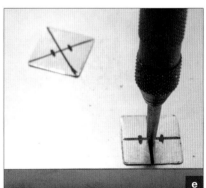

materials
- 2" x 4" 24-gauge patterned brass sheet
- ¾" square of 24-gauge etched copper

tools
- BASIC TOOL KIT **PG.8**
- #52 drill bit
- Beeswax (or cut lube)
- Jeweler's saw and #1 blade
- Pin vise (or flex shaft)
- Steel ring mandrel
- Wooden dapping block and punch

Ring sizing Chart
Use the chart below to estimate the length of strip of metal needed to make a specific size ring.

Ring Size	Circumference in inches	Strip Length
5	2"	2½"
5½	2"	2½"
6	2¹⁄₁₆"	2⁹⁄₁₆"
6½	2¹⁄₁₆"	2⁹⁄₁₆"
7	2⅛"	2⅝"
7½	2⅛"	2⅝"
8	2¼"	2¾"
8½	2¼"	2¾"
9	2⅜"	2⅞"
9½	2⅜"	2⅞"
10	2½"	3"
10½	2½"	3"

TIP **Use a steel ring mandrel, and you can maintain the size of the ring and rivet directly on the ring mandrel.**

1. Measure a ¼" x 4" strip and a ¾" square on the backside of the brass sheet. Mark using a permanent marker. Measure a ¾" square on the etched copper sheet and mark using a permanent marker **(a)**.

2. Using metal shears, cut out the squares and strip **(Techniques, p. 98) (b)**.

3. Rest the squares and the strip on a bench pin. Using a metal file, round the corners and smooth the edges **(Techniques, p. 100) (c)**.

4. With a ruler, draw from corner to corner on the brass square. Draw from center to center on the copper square; measure ⅛" from the center and mark on one of the lines using a permanent marker **(d)**.

5. Make a divot at the center where the lines intersect in both pieces using a center punch and a steel bench block **(e)**.

6. Drill a hole at each divot using the pin vise (or flex shaft) and #52 drill bit **(Techniques, p. 98) (f)**.

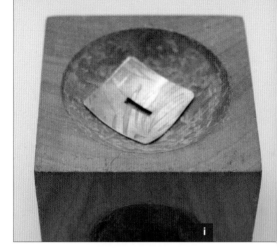

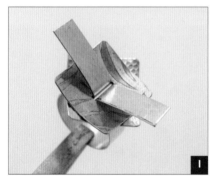

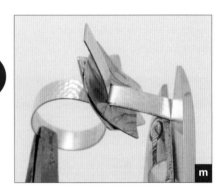

7. Lubricate the saw blade with beeswax (or cut lube), then thread the blade through one hole and pierce a slot between the ⅛" marks approximately ¹⁄₁₆" wide; repeat with the other square **(Techniques, p. 104) (g)**.

8. Using the flat needle file, clean up the pierced slots **(h)**.

9. Lay each square, patterned side facing up, in the wooden dapping block and dome slightly using the large punch **(Techniques, p. 98) (i)**.

10. Wrap the brass strip around the ring mandrel centered at the desired size. Using flatnose pliers, bend the tails up at a 90-degree angle **(j)**.

11. Holding the tails together, thread on the brass square and then the copper square **(k)**.

12. Spread the tails apart, making sure the squares are snug against the bends in the ring shank **(l)**.

13. Using the metal shears, trim the tails to ¾" **(m)**. File and sand to round the cut ends.

14. With the metal shears, thinly slice the tails. This will cause the brass to curl **(n)**.

TIP **File or sand any pointed spots after cutting the tails, as the narrow strips will be sharp.**

15. Using roundnose pliers, snug the curls against the copper square **(o)**.

16. Spray the curls with sealant.

Pierced Brooch

This simple pierced brooch will allow you to customize a pattern that will be sawed from a piece of copper. An integrated pin stem will complete the project. Choose a pattern that has clean lines and not many details for your first project.

Skills
drilling
filing & sanding
making a pin stem
piercing
riveting

materials

- 2" x 3" 24-gauge copper sheet
- 6" 18-gauge bronze wire
- 2 $^1/_{16}$" x $^5/_{16}$" flat-head copper rivets

tools

- BASIC TOOL KIT **PG.8**
- 1.25mm hole punch pliers
- #52 drill bit
- Beeswax (or cut lube)
- Jeweler's saw with #1 blade
- Paper pattern of your choice
- Pin vise (or flex shaft)
- Tacky Glue

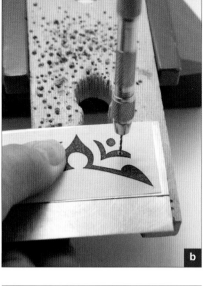

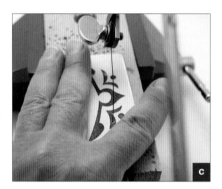

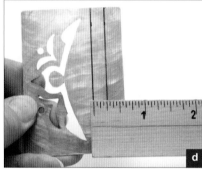

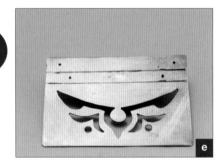

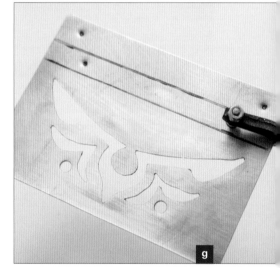

1. Roughup the copper with 600-grit sandpaper. Rinse and dry the sheet. Measure $^5/_8$" from the top and draw a horizontal line with a marker. Make sure your pattern does not extend into this area.

2. Using Tacky Glue, adhere the paper pattern to the copper below the marked line. Set it aside to dry **(a)**.

3. Using a #52 drill bit in the pin vise (or flex shaft), drill a hole in the pattern **(Techniques, p. 98) (b)**.

4. Using a jeweler's saw, thread the lubricated blade through the hole and pierce out your pattern **(Techniques, p. 104) (c)**.

5. Soak the copper in warm water to loosen the adhesive. Wash the copper with mild dish soap and dry the sheet.

6. Using needle files and 600-grit sandpaper, smooth any rough edges **(Techniques, p. 100)**.

7. Measure ¼" up from the $^5/_8$" line and make a horizontal line with the permanent marker **(d)**.

8. In the top section, measure and mark ¼" from each end. Center the marks in each section.

9. In the ¼" area, measure and mark ½" from each end **(e)**.

10. Use the center punch and steel bench block to make a divot at each location **(f)**.

11. Using a 1.8mm hole punch, punch the holes in the second section **(Techniques, p. 99) (g)**.

12. Using a 1.25mm hole punch, punch the holes in the top section **(h)**.

13. Using flatnose pliers, make a 90-degree bend toward the back of the piece at the top line **(i)**.

14. Using flatnose pliers, make a 90-degree bend ½" from one end of the bronze wire **(j)**.

15. Thread the end through one of the top holes on the copper piece.

16. Make a mark on the wire at the second hole location **(k)**.

17. Bend the wire 90 degrees at the mark and thread the wire through the holes **(l)**.

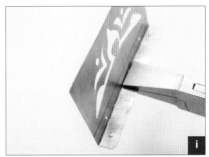
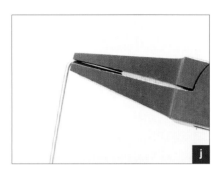

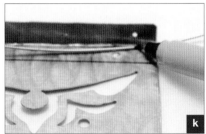

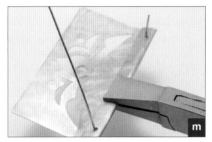

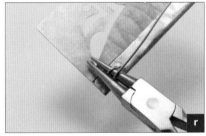
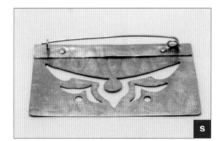

18. Using flatnose pliers, finish bending the top secetion down, capturing the bronze wire **(m)**.

19. From the front side, punch the rivet holes through the bottom section using a 1.8mm hole punch **(n)**.

20. Insert one rivet, flat side on the front. Trim it to ¹⁄₁₆" and set the rivet using the chasing hammer on a steel bench block **(Techniques, p. 101) (o)**.

21. Using roundnose pliers, make a downward facing 'U' bend in the short tail of the wire. This will serve as the catch **(p)**.

22. Grab the long end of the pin stem approximately ¼" from where it exits the copper and make a 90-degree bend towards the catch **(q)**.

23. Using your roundnose pliers, make a 360-degree loop **(r)**.

24. Curve the pin stem wire slightly and tuck it under the catch.

25. Trim the wire to approximately ¹⁄₈" beyond the catch **(s)**. Release the wire and open up the bend slightly.

26. Lay the trimmed end on your bench pin. Using the needle file, file the wire to a sharp point. Turn the wire as necessary to insure the point will be even **(t)**.

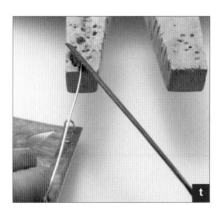

CHALLENGE PROJECT

Hinged Bangle

I feel this project is a bit of a challenge, as it contains more layout, additional sawing, and making hinges. Learning to make hinges will be a great addition to your metalworking skill set. Since the bracelet hinges, it is not necessary to fit the bracelet to your arm.

Skills
drilling
piercing
riveting
sawing
using a mandrel

materials
- 1½" x 12" 24-gauge copper, plain or pre-texturized
- ⁵⁄₃₂" length copper tubing
- ⅛" length copper tubing
- **15** ¹⁄₁₆" x ⁵⁄₁₆" flat-head copper rivets
- 2" small chain
- Copper lobster claw clasp
- **2** 10mm copper jump rings

tools
- BASIC TOOL KIT PG.8
- ⁷⁄₃₂" drill bit
- 2.3mm dapping punch
- #52 drill bit
- #60 drill bit
- Ball-peen hammer
- Beeswax (or cut lube)
- Pin vise (or flex shaft)
- Jeweler's saw with #1 blade
- Narrow needle file
- Rawhide mallet
- Soup can or 2" round dowel
- Spring clamp

TIP **This particular bracelet is a size 7½". You can adjust the size to your preference by adjusting the measurements on your strips of copper.**

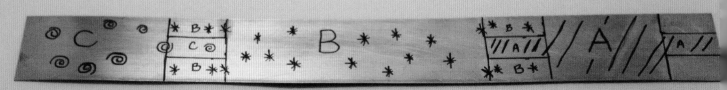

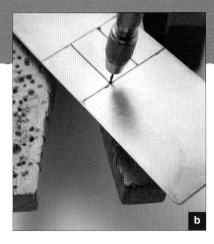

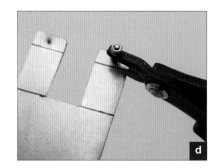

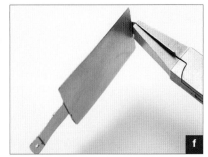

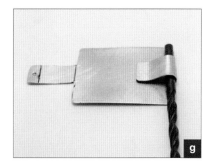

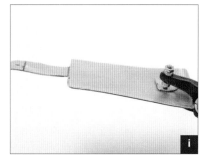

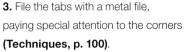

Prepare the hinge tab pattern directly onto the copper sheet as follows: Measure 2½", 3½", 5½", 8", 9", and 11" from one end of the copper sheet. Mark and draw lines using a marker to divide the sheet into six sections.

1. Divide the width of the bracelet into three ½" sections within the 1" sections. These will form your hinge tabs. Label the sections A, B, C as shown. (Note: Symbols on sections are for reference only and should not appear on the finished product.) **(a)**

2. Using a pin vise (or flex shaft) and a #60 drill bit, drill holes and pierce the inside corners that form the hinge tabs. Cut out the tabs on sections C and B **(Techniques, p. 104) (b)**. Repeat to cut out the remaining tabs on section B and A. (Note: Sections A and C have single tabs; section B has two tabs on each end.)

3. File the tabs with a metal file, paying special attention to the corners **(Techniques, p. 100)**.

4. Measure ¼" from the edges of the hinge tabs and draw a line using the permanent marker. Make a mark ⅛" from the edge for the rivet holes **(c)**.

5. Center punch a divot at each mark and then punch the rivet holes using a 1.8mm hole punch **(d)**.

6. On section A, using a jeweler's saw and blade, remove the two outer ½" pieces forming a tab. Trim tab to ¾", file edges smooth and slightly rounded **(e)**.

7. Using flatnose pliers, bend the tab 90 degrees **(f)**.

8. Bend the tab around a 7/32" drill bit **(g)**.

9. At approximately ¼", make another 45-degree bend. Press the tab flat **(h)**.

10. Mark two rivet holes ⅛" from each side of the tab. Make a divot using a 1.8mm center punch **(i)**.

11. Insert and set rivets with the flat side against the tab **(Techniques, p. 101) (j)**.

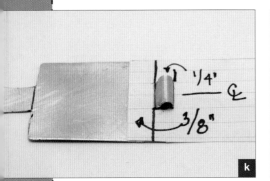

k

l

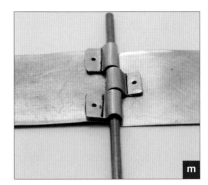

m

n

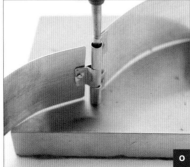

o

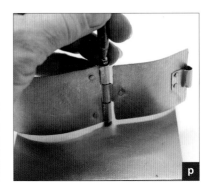

p

12. Make a paper pattern of section C; measure ⅜" from the edge and ½" from either side. Draw a ¼" wide slot as shown. Test fit over the tab on section A to enure a good fit. File the edges **(k)**.

13. Transfer measurements onto the flat end of section C.

14. Using a #60 drill bit and pin vise (or flex shaft) drill a piercing hole within the slot. Using a jeweler's saw and blade, cut out the rectangle. File the inside edges smooth **(Techniques, p. 100)**.

15. Using flatnose pliers, make a 45-degree bend at the ¼" marks. Continue to bend the hinge tabs around the 7⁄32" mandrel and press the tabs flat. All of the hinge tabs should curve toward the inside of the piece, except for section A. That tab should be formed in the opposite direction of the catch end **(l)**.

16. Test fit your hinges by sliding one set together and temporarily pinning using a length of 5⁄32" copper tubing **(m)**.

17. Reinstall the 7⁄32" drill bit and the spring clamp to hold one tab at a

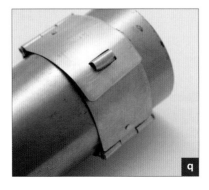

q

r

time in place; punch the body of the bracelet (using the holes in the tab as a guide) with a 1.8mm hole punch. Insert and set rivets.

18. Form bracelet strips into semi-circular pieces using a soup can **(n)**.

19. Slide a length of 5⁄32" tubing through the hinge tabs. Mark ⅛" beyond the last tab and cut the tube to the correct length. File the ends flat if necessary **(o)**.

20. Reinstall the tubing and flare one end using the center punch. Flip the bracelet over and begin flaring the opposite end **(p)**.

21. Complete the flaring using a 2.3mm dapping punch and chasing hammer.

22. Close the bracelet and slide it over a bracelet mandrel, shaping it into a circle with a rawhide mallet **(q)**.

23. For the keeper, cut a piece of ⅛" tubing 1⅜" long. Flatten both ends and round off using a metal file. Drill holes in each end using a #52 drill bit and a pin vise (or a flex shaft). Attach a jump ring and the chain to one end. On the other end of the chain, attach a jump ring and the lobster claw clasp **(r)**.

techniques

Common Techniques

Cutting with Metal Shears

There are many kinds of metal shears on the market; your choice will depend on how they feel as you are using them. They range from a basic style with loop handles to cushioned handles that operate by squeezing them in the same manner as using pliers or wire cutters. I prefer the cushioned handles as they seem to alleviate hand fatigue. In addition, choosing a pair with narrow blades is perfect for more detailed work.

You may be more comfortable starting out using shears to cut shapes instead of using a jeweler's saw. However, do keep in mind shears have their limitations, such as they cannot be used for piercing. Used simply as "open and shut," make sure you turn the metal and not the shears themselves. Also, do not push them completely closed when cutting as the action at the end of the blades when squeezed completely shut may cause a jagged edge.

Texturizing

There are many ways to texturize material: Nail sets, dapping punches, cross-peen hammers, and specialty hammers with interchangeable heads. You can customize hammers, use a rolling mill, and even etch your metal. Texturizing adds a little extra to your piece; it can be located on the exterior or act as a hidden detail. Applying a patina such as liver of sulfur will bring out the texture, adding another element of depth to a piece.

Dapping

Most of the projects in this book call for a wooden dapping block. If you are dapping an etched piece, definitely use a wooden block and dapping punches, as they are more forgiving than a steel block and will not damage the etching.

Thinner metal can be dapped easily. Use steel dapping punches when scratching will not be a problem. Be careful about expecting a hammered or textured piece of metal to have the ability to be dapped. Also remember that hammering work-hardens the metal, making it more resistant to dapping.

Drilling

TIP **One important safety factor to adhere to when drilling is to wear eye protection. Filings and even a broken drill bit may become airborne, threatening your vision.**

Drilling can be performed using a hand-held pin vise, but many artists prefer using a flex shaft. There are some economical flex shafts on the market that are a great investment if you are just starting out. Make sure that you maintain it per the manufacturer's instructions to ensure a long life. The process of drilling is a smooth, fluid one. Like sawing, too much pressure applied on the bit will result in dull and broken bits and distorted holes.

TIP **Using beeswax (or cut lube) will keep the bit cooler and add life to it.**

When you determine the correct size hole for your application, choose a drill bit a size smaller and work your way up. Doing this will ensure you will not bind the bit if it is too big to go through the first time, and will allow you to reassess the hole size. It's always best to start small when you drill the hole, as you cannot add material back in if you misjudged. Burrs created by drilling are easily removed with a drill bit that is 3-4 times larger than the hole. Holding the bit in your hand, carefully twist the larger bit on the drilled hole to gently shave off the burrs.

Hole Punching

As an alternative to drilling, many holes can be punched with special hole-punching pliers. These are great tools to have and are available in different sizes. To start, choose a size to fit your needs; a 1.8mm punch works perfect for a 1/16" shank rivet. They do have their limitations, so make sure you have drill bits on hand to accommodate hard-to-reach holes or thicker material.

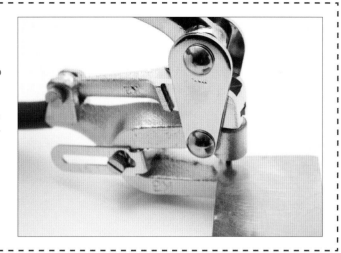

12-Volt Etching

This method of etching is my favorite. It is done using a solution of saturated salt water, two wire leads, and a 12-volt battery. It needs to be carried out in a well-ventilated area; for instance, under an exhaust hood or outside. This method is especially effective on thicker gauge copper (18- and 20-gauge), but also works great on 22- and 24-gauge. A resist is applied to a piece of copper. The resist may be vinyl stickers if you have a particular pattern in mind or you can make your own design by cutting a pattern after applying electrical tape or contact paper to the copper. If there is a copyright-free pattern you want to use, but don't want to attempt it free-hand, print it out and use some Tacky Glue to adhere it to the tape or contact paper. You can then use a craft knife to cut the pattern out; remember the tape serves as the resist—where the tape remains, the copper will not be affected by the etching process. When the salt and water solution is spent, simply add some baking soda to neutralize it and dispose of it.

1. Make lead wires by stripping approximately ¼" of insulation off the wires on each end. Crimp the wire terminations and add alligator clips to each end of the wires.

TIP **You may wish to wrap the crimped terminations with a few layers of electrical tape. This will insulate the wires. If you choose not to wrap them, be sure to wear a pair of lightweight cotton gloves, as the wires will become warm during use.**

2. Measure ¼ cup of water and add 1 tablespoon of salt; stir to dissolve.
3. Cut small pieces of cotton fabric such as a plain white [not terry cloth] towel or an old t-shirt, and then set aside.
4. Clean the copper with a 600-grit sandpaper.
5. Apply the electrical tape resist to the copper without overlapping the strips or pieces.

6. Prepare the paper pattern and use Tacky Glue to secure it to the tape. Using a craft knife, cut out the parts of the pattern you wish to see etched.
7. Once the cutting is completed, remove the paper pattern. Make sure the tape is secure on the copper.
8. Plug one lead onto the positive terminal of the battery. Using the same wire, clamp the alligator clip onto the copper.
9. Plug the other wire onto the negative terminal of the battery. Wad up a piece of the cotton fabric and clamp it into the alligator clip.
10. Dip the cotton into the salt water solution and press it onto the exposed copper. Almost immediately, you will begin to see the electrical etching process; rinse/dip the cotton as needed to keep it wet. Move it around to all exposed areas to ensure a good etch. Replace the fabric piece often, as it will become clogged with residual solution and metal.

materials
- Copper sheet
- Cotton fabric
- Printed pattern
- 1 tbsp. salt
- ¼ c. water

tools
- BASIC TOOL KIT PG.8
- 600-grit sandpaper
- 12-volt battery
- **2** 20" pieces of 16-gauge jacketed stranded speaker wire
- **2** crimp wire terminations to fit the battery terminals
- **2** crimp alligator clips
- Craft knife
- Electrical tape
- Lightweight cotton gloves
- Small disposable plastic container
- Tacky Glue
- Wire crimper
- Wire stripper

11. When you are satisfied with the results, rinse the metal. Remove the tape resist and clean it with a degreasing solution.

Filing & Sanding

Although sometimes tedious, filing is a necessary step in the process of finishing. It is helpful to have assorted sizes of files. Again, if you are starting out, you need not make a huge investment in files. A basic needle file set that includes a flat and half round file from your local home improvement store is perfect.

TIP **Always support your work when filing; "air filing" is not effective, can distort your piece, and can be dangerous. Move your file in one direction; a sanding stick may be moved back and forth.**

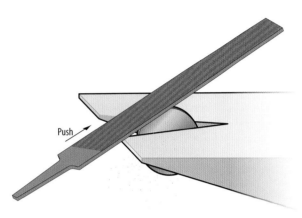

Push

Homemade sanding sticks are also great to have for sanding. To make a batch of sanding sticks, lay a piece of sandpaper face down on a flat surface. Using regular white glue, glue popsicle sticks onto the paper, spacing approximately ⅛" apart. Place a piece of wax paper over the top and weigh down the sticks with a book until dry. Cut the sticks apart; on the back side, use a permanent marker to indicate the grit of each stick.

Inserting Eyelets

1. Prepare the material or materials you will be installing the eyelet into by drilling or punching ⅛" holes **(a)**.
2. Insert the eyelet, lay the metal (or other material) on a steel bench block with the finished side of the eyelet on the bench block.
3. Hold a spring-loaded center punch vertical on the eyelet and push down once **(b)**.
4. Finish setting the eyelet with a chasing hammer. A light touch will help to keep splitting to a minimum (or maybe no splitting at all) **(c)**.

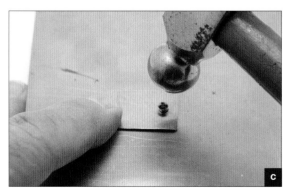

Riveting

Riveting is a necessary skill to master. However, all projects using rivets have detailed process photos.

materials

- Flat-head rivets

tools

- BASIC TOOL KIT
- Chasing hammer
- Drill bit
- Flex shaft (or pin vise)
- Flush cutters
- Hole punch (optional)
- Metal file
- Nail set

Flat-Head Rivets

1. Prepare the materials that will be connected using punched or drilled holes.
2. Insert the rivet with the flat head seated on the side that will be exposed.
3. Holding the rivet head with your thumb, trim the shank to approximately $1/16$" with flush cutters. File the end flat.
4. Position the flat head of the rivet on a steel bench block and lightly hammer the cut end with a chasing hammer. Gently tap the rivet in a circular motion until the end mushrooms over and is flush against the surface.

Round-Head Rivets

1. Prepare the materials that will be connected using punched or drilled holes.
2. Insert the rivet with the round head seated on the side that will be exposed.
3. Holding the rivet head with your thumb, trim the shank to approximately $1/16$" with flush cutters. File the end flat.
4. Secure a $3/32$" nail set (cup-side facing up) in a bench vise.
5. Rest the round head of the rivet on the nail set.
6. Lightly hammer the shank using a chasing hammer.

materials

- Tubing

tools

- BASIC TOOL KIT
- Ball-peen hammer
- Dapping punch
- Drill bit (same size as the tubing)
- Flex shaft (or pin vise)
- Flush cutters
- Jeweler's saw with #1 blade

Tube Rivets

There are specific tools available to expedite the setting of tube rivets. However, before you make the decision to invest in them, try this method using a few simple tools. I find it easier to keep a few different sizes of tubing on hand to make my own rivets. Pre-made tube rivets will almost always need to be cut to length, so it makes sense to make your own.

1. Match your tubing with the appropriate drill bit and drill your hole.
2. Slide the tubing length through the hole and mark the proper length with a permanent marker.

TIP **A rule of thumb is $1/2$" the diameter of tube extending beyond each edge of the "sandwich."**

3. Remove and cut the tubing to the correct length with your jeweler's saw and a #1 blade. Flatten the ends if necessary with a flat file.
4. Secure a center punch in your vise.
5. Reinstall the tube rivet and set it over the point of the center punch.
6. Place the dapping punch inside the tubing and lightly tap it with a ball-peen hammer. When it begins to flare, carefully flip the piece over and repeat. Flip the piece over again and continue to set using your ball-peen hammer. Flip again to flare the opposite side. Continue until you have nicely flared each side and your rivet is secure.

Patina methods

*Ammonia and Salt

Fuming a piece of jewelry — patinating the metal by exposing it to just the fumes of a chemical patina — might sound complicated. But this technique doesn't require a large specialized setup, though you will, of course, need adequate ventilation.

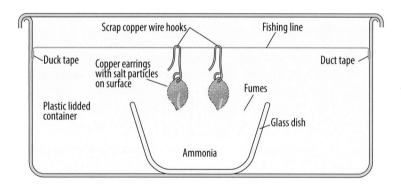

Scrap copper wire hooks
Fishing line
Duck tape
Copper earrings with salt particles on surface
Duct tape
Fumes
Plastic lidded container
Glass dish
Ammonia

materials
- Ammonia
- Clear urethane spray or other sealant
- Plain uniodized salt: table, sea, or kosher
- White vinegar

tools
- Degreasing solution
- Fishing line or duct tape
- Plastic container with tight fitting lid
- Small glass dish to fit inside the plastic container
- Wooden dowel

You can easily create a "fuming tent" (a device to hold the patina's fumes), with just a simple, lidded plastic container and a glass dish. The patination liquid goes into the glass dish, the dish goes into the plastic container, and your prepared piece of jewelry is suspended above the liquid. Once you snap on the lid to capture the fumes, all you have to do is wait for the chemical reaction to cause the patina to appear. Simple.

1. Select the metal you want to patinate. You can use this method to patinate any copper-based metal, such as copper, bronze, brass, or sterling silver.

2. Drill a hole in the metal. (I prefer to fume my pieces after I've drilled an earring wire hole. Then, I can simply thread scrap wire through the hole to suspend the piece above the patina.) If you don't want to drill a hole through your metal, you'll need to wrap scrap wire around it or find another way to hang it.
3. Pickle the metal: Mix a solution of two parts white vinegar to one part plain (non-iodized) salt in a non-metal container. Submerge your metal in this pickle solution and leave it there while you prepare the fuming container.
4. Prepare the fuming container: In a well-ventilated area, pour a small amount of ammonia into a small glass dish so the liquid is approximately ¼" deep. Place the glass dish in a plastic, lidded container.

5. Devise a way to suspend your pieces above the glass dish without letting them touch the liquid. (You can use duct tape to secure fishing line taut across the container or you can wedge a dowel against opposite sides of the container.) Close the lid tightly to capture the fumes.
6. Clean the metal: Check your metal for firescale. If any remains, keep the metal in the pickle until the metal is firescale-free. Then, remove the metal and use a toothbrush and dish soap to scrub it thoroughly. At this point, I like to spray the metal piece with degreasing spray to remove any remaining residue. Rinse the metal thoroughly with plain water. The water should sheet off the metal; if it beads up, you need to clean the metal more thoroughly.

TIP **Once the metal is clean, handle it only by its edges, because the oil from your fingers will affect the patina.**

7 While the metal is still wet, sprinkle plain salt, sea salt, or kosher salt on it. The shape, size, and amount of salt you use will affect the final patina. Experiment to develop your personal preferences.

8. Fume the metal: Suspend the salted piece of metal in the container so it hangs over the dish of ammonia. Make sure the metal does not touch the ammonia. Close the container's lid tightly. Leave the metal in the closed container for at least 15 minutes. Check on the metal periodically to see how the patina is developing. When the metal is your desired color, carefully remove it from the container.

9. Clean the metal and protect the patina. Using dish soap and an old toothbrush, thoroughly wash the metal to remove any ammonia residue and salt. Let the metal air dry.

TIP **Be sure to check with your local authorities regarding the best way to dispose of the remaining ammonia. In most cases you should be able to dilute it with water and pour it down a non-septic-system drain.**

10. Protect the patina's colors. When the metal is completely dry, apply two to three light coats of a clear, urethane spray in a well-ventilated area. This will also halt the patination progress.

*Liver of Sulfur

Liver of sulfur is a simple and relatively safe chemical patina for giving color to a variety of common, non-ferrous jewelry-making metals. It's easy to use, and the range of colors give depth and contrast to your pieces.

Forms

Rocklike chunks are the most common form. Large chunks need to be broken into smaller, pea-sized pieces before using. They are susceptible to moisture and light and so must be kept dry and tightly sealed.

Liquid has a relatively short shelf life and deteriorates quickly.

Gel has the longest shelf life and is easy to use.

Colors

Liver of sulfur progresses through a range of colors as it reaches gray/black. The colors you can achieve and the rate at which you progress through those colors depends on three things: the strength of the solution, the temperature of the solution and the rinse water, and the time your piece sits in the solution. A warmer solution will patinate the metal more quickly than a cool solution: A stronger solution faster than a weak solution: A quick dip more slowly than letting your piece sit for a few seconds. Combine those variables, and you can achieve a wide range of colors.

Regardless of how quickly you move through the colors, they appear in the same order: gold and amber; reddish brown and pink; purples; blues and blue-greens; and finally, gray/black. You can stop the patina at any point by rinsing your piece well in fresh water and then rinsing it in a baking soda and water bath.

How to Use

Clean your metal thoroughly. Pour warm-to-hot distilled water into a glass container. Add liver of sulfur to the water, and stir it until it's dissolved (chunks) or evenly mixed (gel). (Liquid liver of sulfur doesn't need to be diluted.)

There's no set-in-stone rule for how strong to mix the solution, but a good place to start is a pea-size (or equivalent) amount of liver of sulfur to 1 cup of water. The solution should be light yellow with a greenish undertone.

Use copper or steel tongs to dip your piece in the liver of sulfur solution for a second or two, rinse in fresh water, and then scrub it with a brass brush and soapy water. Rinse your piece in fresh water to remove any soap residue and dip it in the solution again. Repeat until you reach your desired color.

TIP **If you don't want the entire piece to have a patina, use a soft paintbrush or cotton swab to apply the liver of sulfur solution to select areas.**

Build the patina up slowly. This takes longer, but makes the patina more durable, and you have more control over the final color. Use fine-grit sandpaper steel wool to remove the patina from the high points as desired.

Piercing

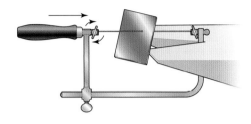

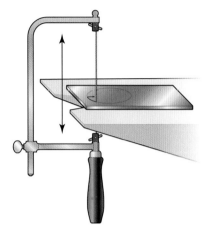

Metal piercing chart

B&S METAL GAUGE	IDEAL BLADE SIZE	DRILL BIT #
26 (0.4 mm)	8/0	80
24–26 (0.5–0.4 mm)	7/0	80
24–26 (0.5–0.4 mm)	6/0	79
22–24 (0.6–0.5 mm)	5/0	78
22–24 (0.6–0.5 mm)	4/0	77
22 (0.6 mm)	3/0	76
20–22 (0.8–0.6 mm)	2/0	75
20–22 (0.8–0.6 mm)	1/0	73
18–20 (1.0–0.8 mm)	1	71
18–20 (1.0–0.8 mm)	2	70
16–18 (1.3–1.0 mm)	3	68
16–18 (1.3–1.0 mm)	4	67
14–16 (1.6–1.3 mm)	5	65
12–16 (2.1–1.3 mm)	6	58
12–14 (2.1–1.6 mm)	7	57
12 (2.1 mm)	8	55

(Smallest → Largest)

Piercing refers to removing material without making exterior cuts. Drill a hole inside the shape you want to remove that matches the size of the blade you are using. (See chart to properly match bits with blade size.) Release one end of the blade from the saw frame (the bottom is usually the easiest). Thread the blade through the hole, making sure the design is facing up. Support the metal piece so it doesn't push the end of the blade out of alignment and tighten the blade in the frame.

Test the blade for tension **(above left)**. Pierce your design, staying on the inside of the line **(above right)**. Keep the original line so you can file the top later to create an even edge. The sawn piece will fall from the sheet once you've completed the cut.

Sawing

I always thought it was easier to use shears to cut shapes because I was a bit leery of using the jeweler's saw. However, I have since discovered how easy it is to use the saw; the metal will stay straight and true and the edges will be smoother. There are times when using shears are great; I find them perfect for small pieces that can easily be flattened out with a single tap from a chasing hammer in the event they distort during cutting. Larger pieces are not so easy to flatten consistently; that is when the saw comes into play. You do not have to make a big investment in a saw frame, but do make sure it is adjustable.

Load your blade in the top slot with the teeth facing down and away from you. Tighten the thumbscrew. Adjust the saw and secure the other end of the blade; slide the frame to put tension on the blade. (You can also adjust the frame so the end of the blade is approximately ⅛" from the bottom slot, then compress the saw and secure the end of the blade.) A good way to tell if your tension is good is to pluck the blade. You should hear a high pitched sound that reverberates. If you hear a dull thump, tighten the blade.

Rest your work on a solid bench pin, preferably with a 'v' slot. Hold your saw frame at a 90-degree angle to your work. Begin sawing making sure to use the entire length of your blade for each stroke. Try not to apply too much force on the blade; let the blade do the work. This will ensure smooth fluid strokes (and fewer broken blades). When you get to a corner, keep the blade moving and

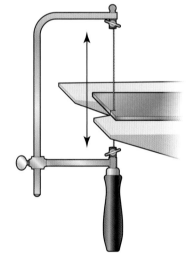

ease it into the corner by moving the saw frame as well as moving the metal.

If your piece allows for it, position your fingers pointing away from your body in a 'v' formation; with one finger on either side of your blade. No matter where your fingers need to be positioned, make sure they are away from the path of your blade. If you feel more comfortable as you are starting out, use a spring clamp to hold your work to the bench pin.

TIP **It is always a good idea to keep beeswax or cutting lube handy to swipe on the blade. This helps keep it cool during use and will also prolong the life of the blade.**

Making Components
Closures

The closure is one, if not the most important part, of a piece of jewelry. It must be as beautiful as the focal, but also a functional entity of the piece as a whole. This is when being able to make your own simple closure comes into play.

The following closures can make good use of scraps if you are lucky enough to have a collection of them. They can also be made using thinner-gauge wire, but take into consideration the integrity of the closure when choosing to use thinner wire, especially for jump rings and hooks.

TIPS
Points to consider when choosing a closure:

Think about the size and the weight of the piece–
- **Is the piece lightweight? If so, a hook and eye closure would be great.**
- **Does the focal or necklace design incorporate heavier objects? A toggle would be perfect in this case.**

Think about the type of closure that will fit the design–
- **A delicate design calls for a delicate closure, just like a chunky design screams for a chunky one.**

Articulating Clasp

This articulating closure is completely cold connected. Designed to swivel, it offers an excellent level of comfort for the wearer.

materials
- 8" 18- or 16-gauge wire

tools
- BASIC TOOL KIT **PG.8**
- 2mm mandrel (a 6" piece of 12-gauge wire works great)
- 10mm mandrel
- Bent nose pliers
- Flush cutters

1. Cut two pieces of wire 1¾" long and two pieces 1½" long. File ends flat with a metal file.
2. Using the tip of roundnose pliers, grasp one end of a 1¾" wire and make a small plain loop **(a)**.
3. Slide the loop over the 2mm mandrel. Hold it with bentnose pliers, and, using your fingers, wrap it 2½ times around the mandrel **(b)**.
4. Keeping the wire on the mandrel, slide it to the tip. With roundnose pliers, grasp the end of the tail and make a plain loop perpendicular to the coil **(c).** Trim the wire.
5. Using the chasing hammer, flatten one end of the 1½" wires. Smooth the flattened end with a 600-grit sanding stick.

6. Thread the flattened wire through the coil starting from the end with the plain loop **(d).**
7. Flatten the end with a chasing hammer on a steel bench block **(e).**
8. Turn up the tip slightly with roundnose pliers **(f).**
9. Using a 10mm mandrel, make a hook in the wire **(g).**

10. Repeat on the other set of wires. When making the 10mm hook, continue to bend it so it forms a plain loop. Trim the end if needed, and squeeze the loop closed.
11. Lay both pieces on the steel bench block and hammer the hooks and loops to flatten and work-harden them **(h).**

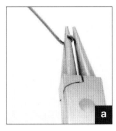
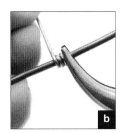

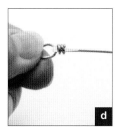

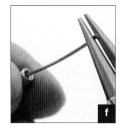

Hook and Eye Clasp

A hook and eye clasp can be used anywhere and marries nicely with leather, ribbon, or chain. It is also great for using up scrap pieces of wire.

materials

- 16-gauge wire

tools

- BASIC TOOL KIT

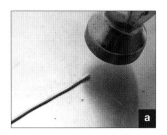

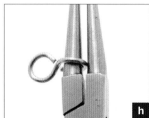

1. Cut one piece of wire 2¾" long and one 1½" long. File the ends flat with a metal file.
2. Hammer the tip on each end of the 2¾" wire using the chasing hammer on the steel bench block **(a)**.
3. Starting with the 2¾" wire, grasp one end with the tip of the roundnose pliers and make a loop. Grasp the other end and make a loop. (The loops should face inward toward each other.) **(b)**

4. Position the pliers against one loop and make a bend toward the center **(c)**.
5. Re-position the pliers against the other loop and make an opposing bend toward the center **(d)**.
6. Lay the hook on the steel bench block and lightly hammer the bends with a chasing hammer to add dimension and to work-harden the metal, creating rigidity **(e)**.

7. Using the 1½" piece of wire, grasp one end with the widest part of the roundnose pliers and make a plain loop **(f)**.
8. Bend the loop back so it is centered on the wire **(g)**.
9. Grasp the other end and make a perpendicular plain loop **(h)**.
10. Lay one plain loop on the steel bench block and slightly hammer it with a chasing hammer to add dimension and to work-harden the metal **(i)**.

Repeat for the second loop.
11. After hammering, use the roundnose pliers to adjust the loops as needed.

Spectacle Links

Spectacle links can be incorporated into many projects.

materials

- 16- or 18-gauge wire

tools

- BASIC TOOL KIT
- Bentnose pliers
- Flush cutters

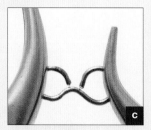

1. Cut the wire to the desired length and file the ends flat with a metal file.
2. Grasp one end using roundnose pliers and make a plain loop; bend the back so it is centered on the wire **(a)**.
3. Grasp the opposite end and make a plain loop perpendicular to the first loop, bringing the two cut ends together **(b)**.
4. Grasp each plain loop with bentnose pliers. Bend the loops toward one another so they are aligned **(c)**.
5. Adjust as necessary to ensure the loops are closed tightly.

Washer Toggle Closure

This toggle closure uses a 1" washer and a shape reminiscent of a Grandfather Clock pendulum. Since the washer is 24-gauge wire, I used reverse Figure-8 links to prevent the washer from becoming detached from the chain or cord. To add continuity, use the same reverse Figure-8 link on the pendulum shape.

materials

- 1" outside diameter (OD) x ½" inside diameter (ID) 24-gauge copper flat washer
- 1½" x 1" 24-gauge copper sheet
- 20" 18-gauge wire (for 10 ¾" links)

tools

- BASIC TOOL KIT PG.8
- Circle pattern
- Needle file
- Rawhide mallet
- Wooden dapping block with punch

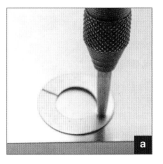
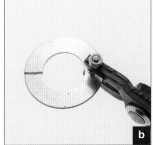
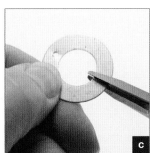
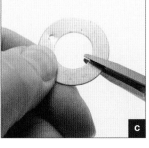

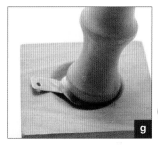

107

1. Mark 12:00 and 6:00 locations on the washer.
2. Use a center punch to make a divot on one side **(a)**.
3. Make a hole punch with the 1.8mm punch at the divot **(Techniques, p. 99) (b)**.
4. On the opposing side, cut a thin slit in the washer with metal shears, making sure not to remove too much material **(c)**.

5. Carefully round the inner and outer cut edges with a needle file.
6. Hammer the washer with a rawhide mallet on a steel bench block to work-harden it.
7. Trace a ⅝" circle on the copper sheet, then draw a tab ¼" wide x ½" long **(d)**.
8. Cut out the pendulum using metal shears **(Techniques, p. 98) (e)**.

9. File the edges using a metal file, and refine with a 600-grit sanding stick **(Techniques, p.100).**
10. Use a center punch to make a divot in the smaller side of the pendulum; then use a 1.8mm punch to make a hole at the divot **(f)**.
11. Lay the circular end in the wooden dapping block and dome slightly **(g)**.

12. Attach reverse Figure-8 links to each piece **(Techniques, p.109) (h)**.
13. Insert the solid circle part of the toggle assembly into the washer. It may need to be adjusted slightly in order to lay flat **(i)**.

Make Your Own Earring Wire Tool

Mastering making your own earring wires is a must-have skill. Not only will you be able to make basic earring wires, you will be able to customize them to accentuate your design. While there are many tools available for making earring wires, I found that modifying different size interlocking blocks gives me many options. I use blocks with 27mm, 18mm, and 10mm posts.

1. Mark ¹⁄₁₆" off the edge of two posts on each block. Drill a hole with the #54 bit. Install one microbolt per hole from the bottom up. Thread a hex nut onto the bolt and tighten by using a slotted screwdriver on the bottom and tightening the hex nut with bentnose pliers. Glue with cyanoacrylate glue to secure.

2. On the 27mm and 18mm posts, mark a 12mm long slot; on the 10mm post, mark an 8mm slot with the permanent marker, keeping close to the screw. Using the utility knife, cut out the slot. The slot will allow a place for the bead to rest while completing the bend in the wire.

materials

- 10, 18, and 27mm posts
- Various sized interlocking blocks
- 5 0-80 x ½" slotted flat-head microbolt and hex nut

tools

- BASIC TOOL KIT **PG.8**
- #54 drill bit
- Bentnose pliers
- Small slotted screwdriver
- Craft knife

Earring Wires

1. Cut two pieces of wire 2" long. Use a metal file to round the ends. Grasp one end of the wire with the roundnose pliers and make a 4mm plain loop. Repeat with the second wire **(a)**.

2. Using a cup bur, round the end of the earring wire **(b)**.

3. Slide the loop over the microbolt in the 10mm interlocking block. Using your fingers, curve the wire around the peg, upturning the end slightly. Remove and repeat with a second wire **(c)**.

4. To make a variation, prepare a 3½" earring wire and bend it around the 27mm block. Position the curve in a pair of ring-bending pliers and apply light pressure **(d)**.

Bead-embellished earring wires

1. Cut two pieces of wire 2½" long. Use a cup bur to round the ends. Grasp one end of the wire with the roundnose pliers and make a 4mm plain loop. Repeat with the second wire.

2. Slide an 8 or 10mm bead on the wire, then slide the loop over the microbolt on the 18 or 27mm interlocking block. Position the bead in the cut out **(e)**.

3. Use your fingers to curve the wire around the peg while holding the bead in the cut out. Upturn the end slightly. Remove and repeat with the second wire **(f)**.

TIP **By slightly adjusing the length of the wire, you can make a longer earring wire to accommodate a number of different dangles.**

materials

- 4" of 20- or 21-gauge silver-plated wire

tools

- BASIC TOOL KIT **PG.8**
- 10mm block or 10mm mandrel (will also need for 18mm and 27mm size)
- Cup bur
- Roundnose pliers

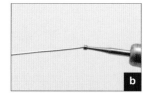

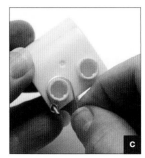

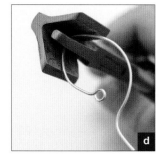

Reverse Figure-8 Links

Reverse Figure-8 links can be incorporated into many projects, from simple closure options to chain making. The size is easily adjusted, and they marry perfectly with jump rings.

materials
• 16- or 18-gauge copper wire

tools
• BASIC TOOL KIT PG.8

A 2" piece of wire will make a ¾" long reverse Figure-8 link with 5mm loops; 2½" piece will make a 1¼" reverse Figure-8 link with 6mm loops; and a 3" piece will make a 1" reverse Figure-8 link with 8mm loops. You can make the loops round or oval, and can hammer the curves flat or leave them round. Hammering the loops will work-harden them, making them stronger and less likely to pull open.

1. Using flush cutters, cut wire to the desired length and file ends flat with a file.
2. Grasp one end using roundnose pliers and make a plain loop **(a)**.
3. Grasp the opposite end and make an opposing loop; then bend the wire **(b)**.
4. Adjust as necessary to ensure the plain loops are tight.

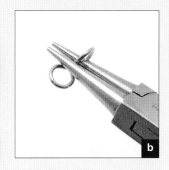

Jump Rings

You can easily make your own jump rings. All you need is wire, a mandrel, and a jeweler's saw or flush cutters. Mandrels can be wooden, plastic, or metal.

materials
• 16- or 18-gauge wire of your choice

tools
• BASIC TOOL KIT PG.8
• Mandrel
• Wire

109

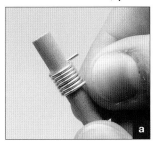

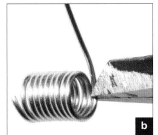

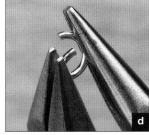

Making jump rings
1. Keeping the wire on the spool, clean a length of wire using 600-grit sandpaper.
2. Select a wooden dowel with a diameter the size matching the inside diameter of the jump rings you want to make. Drill a hole through one end of the dowel. Insert the end of the wire into the hole and tightly coil the wire around the dowel. Holding one end of the wire secure, tightly wrap the wire around the mandrel, making as many wraps as rings needed **(a).**
3. Cut the wire that anchors the coil. Tuck the cut end against the mandrel. Remove coil from mandrel.
4. Holding the flush-cut edge of your wire cutters at a right angle to the coil, trim the wire tail from each end of the coil **(b).**
5. Slightly separate the first ring from the coil. Holding the flush-cut edge of your cutters at a right angle to the wire, cut where the wire completes the first ring **(c)**. To flush-cut the pointed end, flip your cutters over to the flush-cut side, and cut again so both cuts are flush. Continue cutting rings from the coil.
6. After cutting, use two pairs of pliers to grasp the ring on either side of the cut. Wiggle the sides back and forth, eventually closing the gap.
7. When the cut ends snap against each other, you have effectively work-hardened the rings.

Opening and closing a jump ring or loop
Hold the jump ring with two pairs of pliers, such as chain-nose, flatnose, and/or bent-nose. To open the jump ring, bring one pair of pliers toward you, and push the other pair away from you. (Do not pull the jump ring open sideways.) **(d)**

Multi-Strand Neck Wire

Some pieces call for a streamlined look when it comes to hanging. A multi-strand neck wire will showcase a piece without overshadowing it. This basic neck wire is a mix of steel and bronze—simple to make and easy to wear.

materials
- 50" 16-gauge dark, annealed steel wire
- 36" 18-gauge bronze wire

tools
- BASIC TOOL KIT PG.8
- Dish soap
- 12mm mandrel
- Heavy-duty wire cutters
- Renaissance wax
- Scotch Brite pad

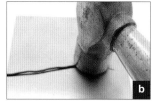

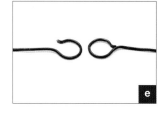
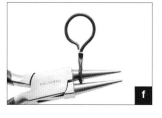

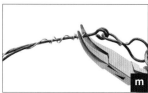

16-gauge dark, annealed steel wire can be found at a home improvement store and comes in a 400-foot roll. Because the bare wire is treated with tool oil, wipe it clean with an absorbent towel. The wire is stiff, but being in a coil helps make the curve needed for the neck wire.

1. Cut the steel wire into two 22" pieces and two 3" pieces (for the clasp). File the ends flat.
2. To add texture, hammer the two neck wires with the ball-peen hammer **(a)**.
3. Using the flat face of the ball-peen hammer, flatten each end of the clasp wires to approximately ¼" **(b)**. Use the metal file to smooth the ends.
4. Using a 12mm mandrel, make a plain loop in one end of each clasp **(c)**.

5. With roundnose pliers, slightly upturn the short ends **(d)**.
6. Leave the loop open on one clasp wire (this will be the clasp hook) and close the other loop **(e)**.
7. Form 6mm loops perpendicular to the 12mm loops. Slightly upturn the ends **(f)**.
8. Press both ends of the 6mm loops flat.
9. With the flat face of your ball-peen hammer, flatten the curve of the loops **(g)**.
10. Adjust as necessary to retain the shape of the plain loops after hammering.
11. Wash all wires with a Scotch Brite pad and soap and water. Dry thoroughly. When dry, apply a coat of Renaissance wax.
12. Grasp the ends of the neck wire and make a 5mm plain loop on one end of each wire **(h)**.

13. Open the loop of the hook. Slide on the two neck wires and close the loop **(i)**.
14. Slide the pendant onto the wires and make a second set of loops. Attach the plain loop closure.
15. Slide the bronze wire through the bail and center the pendant on the neck wire **(j)**.
16. Using your fingers, bend the bronze wire around the neck wires on either side of the pendant, in opposite directions. The pendant will now stay in the center **(k)**.
17. Continue forming the bronze wire around the neck wire, randomly wrapping loose and tight loops. Stop ¾" short of the clasps and trim the bronze wire to 1" long **(l)**.
18. Flatten the bronze wire tails by striking them with the flat face of your ball-peen hammer.

19. Using flatnose pliers, wrap the tails tightly around the neck wires and squeeze to secure **(m)**.
20. Use your fingers to form the neck wires, and secure the clasp. Adjust the tension on the neck wire by gently pulling the neck wires apart.

Acknowledgments

Writing a book, especially your first one, is a truly honorable experience; but it can also cause panic attacks and serious bouts of self-doubt. Therefore, my thanks are many.

A special thank you goes out to my family and friends for their support, patience, understanding and their enthusiasm.

I would also like to thank *Rings & Things*, *Contenti*, *Rio Grande*, *Jay-Cee Rivets,* and *Chain Gallery* for their generous donations that helped make the projects in my book come alive.

Finally, I would like to extend thanks to my Editor, Dianne Wheeler; my Art Director, Lisa Bergman; and William Zuback, my photographer who created the amazing beauty shots.

About the Author

Judy Freyer Thompson has been creating for 10 years. Mostly self-taught, she is an artist with a background in such diverse fields as aerospace, mechanical manufacturing and farming. Her jewelry and small sculpture reflect both her experience and fascination with materials that are earthy, and more often than not she likes to 'think outside the box'. Creating with items such as bones, teeth, fur and found objects feeds her desire to design one-of-a-kind pieces of wearable art. Her work has been in various galleries and she has enjoyed the experience of being published in various magazines and books.

This book is dedicated to her husband Mel and daughter Madison. Both have been there through thick and thin. Madison critiqued, advised, and stated 'awesome' for something she really liked.

When she is not creating, she is adventuring with Madison, teaching, and truly enjoys making people laugh and seeing the brighter side of life.

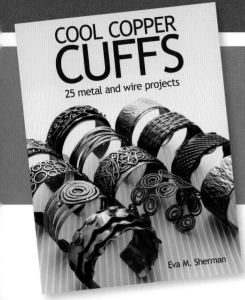

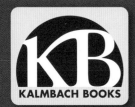